# How To Cross Stitch

## Your Step By Step Guide To Cross Stitching

## Volume 2

**HowExpert with Brenda Morris**

**Copyright HowExpert™**
**www.HowExpert.com**

**For more tips related to this topic, visit HowExpert.com/crossstitch2.**

# Recommended Resources

- HowExpert.com – Quick 'How To' Guides on All Topics from A to Z by Everyday Experts.
- HowExpert.com/free – Free HowExpert Email Newsletter.
- HowExpert.com/books – HowExpert Books
- HowExpert.com/courses – HowExpert Courses
- HowExpert.com/clothing – HowExpert Clothing
- HowExpert.com/membership – HowExpert Membership Site
- HowExpert.com/affiliates – HowExpert Affiliate Program
- HowExpert.com/writers – Write About Your #1 Passion/Knowledge/Expertise & Become a HowExpert Author.
- HowExpert.com/resources – Additional HowExpert Recommended Resources
- YouTube.com/HowExpert – Subscribe to HowExpert YouTube.
- Instagram.com/HowExpert – Follow HowExpert on Instagram.
- Facebook.com/HowExpert – Follow HowExpert on Facebook.

# Publisher's Foreword

Dear HowExpert Reader,

HowExpert publishes quick 'how to' guides on all topics from A to Z by everyday experts.

At HowExpert, our mission is to discover, empower, and maximize talents of everyday people to ultimately make a positive impact in the world for all topics from A to Z...one everyday expert at a time!

All of our HowExpert guides are written by everyday people just like you and me who have a passion, knowledge, and expertise for a specific topic.

We take great pride in selecting everyday experts who have a passion, great writing skills, and knowledge about a topic that they love to be able to teach you about the topic you are also passionate about and eager to learn about.

We hope you get a lot of value from our HowExpert guides and it can make a positive impact in your life in some kind of way. All of our readers including you altogether help us continue living our mission of making a positive impact in the world for all spheres of influences from A to Z.

If you enjoyed one of our HowExpert guides, then please take a moment to send us your feedback from wherever you got this book.

Thank you and we wish you all the best in all aspects of life.

Sincerely,

BJ Min
Founder & Publisher of HowExpert
HowExpert.com

PS...If you are also interested in becoming a HowExpert author, then please visit our website at HowExpert.com/writers. Thank you & again, all the best!

**COPYRIGHT, LEGAL NOTICE AND DISCLAIMER:**

COPYRIGHT © BY HOWEXPERT™ (OWNED BY HOT METHODS). ALL RIGHTS RESERVED WORLDWIDE. NO PART OF THIS PUBLICATION MAY BE REPRODUCED IN ANY FORM OR BY ANY MEANS, INCLUDING SCANNING, PHOTOCOPYING, OR OTHERWISE WITHOUT PRIOR WRITTEN PERMISSION OF THE COPYRIGHT HOLDER.

DISCLAIMER AND TERMS OF USE: PLEASE NOTE THAT MUCH OF THIS PUBLICATION IS BASED ON PERSONAL EXPERIENCE AND ANECDOTAL EVIDENCE. ALTHOUGH THE AUTHOR AND PUBLISHER HAVE MADE EVERY REASONABLE ATTEMPT TO ACHIEVE COMPLETE ACCURACY OF THE CONTENT IN THIS GUIDE, THEY ASSUME NO RESPONSIBILITY FOR ERRORS OR OMISSIONS. ALSO, YOU SHOULD USE THIS INFORMATION AS YOU SEE FIT, AND AT YOUR OWN RISK. YOUR PARTICULAR SITUATION MAY NOT BE EXACTLY SUITED TO THE EXAMPLES ILLUSTRATED HERE; IN FACT, IT'S LIKELY THAT THEY WON'T BE THE SAME, AND YOU SHOULD ADJUST YOUR USE OF THE INFORMATION AND RECOMMENDATIONS ACCORDINGLY.

THE AUTHOR AND PUBLISHER DO NOT WARRANT THE PERFORMANCE, EFFECTIVENESS OR APPLICABILITY OF ANY SITES LISTED OR LINKED TO IN THIS BOOK. ALL LINKS ARE FOR INFORMATION PURPOSES ONLY AND ARE NOT WARRANTED FOR CONTENT, ACCURACY OR ANY OTHER IMPLIED OR EXPLICIT PURPOSE.

ANY TRADEMARKS, SERVICE MARKS, PRODUCT NAMES OR NAMED FEATURES ARE ASSUMED TO BE THE PROPERTY OF THEIR RESPECTIVE OWNERS, AND ARE USED ONLY FOR REFERENCE. THERE IS NO IMPLIED ENDORSEMENT IF WE USE ONE OF THESE TERMS.

NO PART OF THIS BOOK MAY BE REPRODUCED, STORED IN A RETRIEVAL SYSTEM, OR TRANSMITTED BY ANY OTHER MEANS: ELECTRONIC, MECHANICAL, PHOTOCOPYING, RECORDING, OR OTHERWISE, WITHOUT THE PRIOR WRITTEN PERMISSION OF THE AUTHOR.

ANY VIOLATION BY STEALING THIS BOOK OR DOWNLOADING OR SHARING IT ILLEGALLY WILL BE PROSECUTED BY LAWYERS TO THE FULLEST EXTENT. THIS PUBLICATION IS PROTECTED UNDER THE US COPYRIGHT ACT OF 1976 AND ALL OTHER APPLICABLE INTERNATIONAL, FEDERAL, STATE AND LOCAL LAWS AND ALL RIGHTS ARE RESERVED, INCLUDING RESALE RIGHTS: YOU ARE NOT ALLOWED TO GIVE OR SELL THIS GUIDE TO ANYONE ELSE.

THIS PUBLICATION IS DESIGNED TO PROVIDE ACCURATE AND AUTHORITATIVE INFORMATION WITH REGARD TO THE SUBJECT MATTER COVERED. IT IS SOLD WITH THE UNDERSTANDING THAT THE AUTHORS AND PUBLISHERS ARE NOT ENGAGED IN RENDERING LEGAL, FINANCIAL, OR OTHER PROFESSIONAL ADVICE. LAWS AND PRACTICES OFTEN VARY FROM STATE TO STATE AND IF LEGAL OR OTHER EXPERT ASSISTANCE IS REQUIRED, THE SERVICES OF A PROFESSIONAL SHOULD BE SOUGHT. THE AUTHORS AND PUBLISHER SPECIFICALLY DISCLAIM ANY LIABILITY THAT IS INCURRED FROM THE USE OR APPLICATION OF THE CONTENTS OF THIS BOOK.

**COPYRIGHT BY HOWEXPERT™ (OWNED BY HOT METHODS)**
**ALL RIGHTS RESERVED WORLDWIDE.**

# Table of Contents

**Recommended Resources ............................... 2**

**Publisher's Foreword ...................................... 3**

**Introduction ..................................................... 8**
    Brief History of Cross Stitch ..................................... 8
    What the Guide Focuses On ..................................... 11

**Chapter 1: Types of Cross Stitch .................... 12**
    Stamped Cross Stitch ................................................ 12
    Counted Cross Stitch ................................................. 13

**Chapter 2: Materials Used for Cross Stitch .... 15**
    What You Need ......................................................... 15

**Chapter 3: Needles Used for Cross Stitch ...... 16**
    Needle Sizes Matched to Fabric Count Size ............. 19

**Chapter 4: Types of Floss Used for Cross Stitch ........................................................................ 22**
    Strand Count for Cross Stitch & Backstitch for Various Fabric Counts ............................................................ 22

**Chapter 5: Types of Fabrics Used for Cross Stitch ................................................................. 27**
    Aida ............................................................................ 28
    Hardnager (also known as Oslo) ............................... 28
    Anne Cloth ................................................................. 29
    Lady Elizabeth Afghan .............................................. 30
    Lugana ....................................................................... 31
    Linda .......................................................................... 32
    Jobelan ...................................................................... 32
    Jubilee ....................................................................... 33
    Murano ...................................................................... 34
    Belfast Linen ............................................................. 34
    Waste Canvas ............................................................ 35

## Chapter 6: Types of Hoops and frames Used for Cross Stitch ............................................. 36
Clip-on Frames (also known as Q-Snap Frames) .......... 36
Scroll Frames .................................................................. 37
Hoops ............................................................................. 39
Stretcher Bars ................................................................ 40

## Chapter 7: How To prepare the fabric for a Project .................................................................. 41
Preparing Fabric for Stitching ...................................... 41
   STEP-BY-STEP ACTION STEPS ............................... 41

## Chapter 8: How To find the Center Point of the Fabric ................................................................... 43
The First METHOD - Folding ........................................ 43
   Step-By-Step Action Steps ........................................ 43
The Second METHOD - Measuring ............................. 46
   Step-By-Step Action Steps ........................................ 47

## Chapter 9: How To Do Some of The Different Stitches of Cross Stitch ..................................... 50
Threading the Needle ................................................... 50
   Step-By-Step Action Steps ........................................ 50
Cross Stitch (also known as the English Cross stitch or sampler stitch) ................................................................ 54
   Step-By-Step Action Steps ........................................ 54
Quarter-Cross Stitch ..................................................... 57
   Step-By-Step Action Steps ........................................ 57
Three-Quarter Cross Stitch .......................................... 59
   Step-By-Step Action Steps ........................................ 59
Backstitch ...................................................................... 62
   Step-By-Step Action Steps ........................................ 62
Herringbone Stitch ....................................................... 68
   Step-By-Step Action Steps ........................................ 68

Long Stitch/Short Stitch (also known as the Brick stitch) ............................................................................. 72
   Step-By-Step Action Steps ................................. 72
Double Cross Stitch ................................................ 78
   Step-By-Step Action Steps ................................. 78
Smyrna Cross Stitch ............................................... 85
   Step-By-Step Action Steps ................................. 85
Four-sided Stitch .................................................... 91
   Step-By-Step Action Steps ................................. 91
Hungarian Stitch ................................................... 100
   Step-By-Step Action Steps ............................... 100
Algerian Eye Stitch ............................................... 105
   Step-By-Step Action Steps ............................... 105
Eyelet Stitch .......................................................... 115
   Step-By-Step Action Steps ............................... 115
Tent Stitch ............................................................. 132
   Step-By-Step Action Steps ............................... 132
Irish Stitch ............................................................ 141
   Step-By-Step Action Steps ............................... 141
Rice Stitch ............................................................. 151
   Step-By-Step Action Steps ............................... 151

**Chapter 10: How To prepare a project for finishing .................................................. 158**

**Conclusion ..................................................... 161**

**About the Expert ........................................... 162**

**Recommended Resources ........................... 163**

# Introduction

Many people used to consider cross stitch to be a craft that little old ladies did while sitting in their rocking chairs at the old folks' home. Another line of thought was that only people back in the days before electricity and television did it. After all, who would want to do cross stitch when they could be watching TV or playing video games, right? Believe it or not, there have been some famous people who have taken up a stitch or two, like actress Miranda Richardson (*Young Victoria*) and ex-Pittsburgh Steeler "Mean Joe" Greene.

## *Brief History of Cross Stitch*

Evidence of cross stitch in combination with embroidery has been found from as early as 5,000 BC; however, the earliest piece of cross stitch-only fabric was found in a tomb in Upper Egypt which was dated about 500 AD. The dry desert climate helped to preserve the linen material, but examples from other ancient civilizations have been harder to find due to less favorable preservation conditions.

Many historians believe that cross stitch may have begun its development into the craft we know today with the Chinese because of the popularity of detailed embroidery during the T'ang Dynasty (618 AD-906 AD). From there, they believe it moved via trade routes through India and Egypt. Following these trade routes, it continued on to Greece and Rome and then spread throughout the eastern

Mediterranean into the Middle East. Eventually it reached Europe and the British Isles, probably with those returning from the Crusades. Other historians believe that the art followed another route. At any rate, so many designs and stitches have crossed cultural and geographical lines that it is hard to actually determine exactly where the technique started.

Initially, cross stitch was used to embellish clothing and household furnishings such as cushions and drapery among the peasant population. The original patterns tended to be floral or geometric shapes worked in black or red cotton thread on linen fabric. The more embellished items or clothing a person had, the wealthier they were considered to be, and the higher their status in the community.

Each culture developed its own traditional designs or styles. Border patterns differed from culture to culture or even from community to community within a culture. India specializes in cross stitch embroidery with additional items such as beads or sequins on plain fabric, since evenweave fabrics are an uncommon commodity there. Spain introduced a technique called blackwork. The Italians developed a reverse technique called Assisi work.

In 1524, Germany printed the first pattern book and in 1586 France published a pattern leaflet featuring Oriental-inspired designs. Although patterns were being printed, they were not readily available, so when a stitcher would come across a stitch they had not seen before, they would add it to a "sampler cloth". This was usually a narrow strip of linen or other cloth that they used to collect stitches and designs they liked. This is where samplers got their start.

Pre-printed designs on fabric became available in the early 1500s. They were outlines, much like those seen today with stamped cross stitch or embroidery. In 1804 the grid pattern that we know today was introduced. Between 1830 and 1840, the numbers of printed colored cross stitch and canvas charts were at their highest. The craft was so popular that by 1840, 14,000 patterns had been published and sold, which was unbelievable for the time.

All of these techniques and patterns came to the Americas with the settlers. However, since the supplies were not as plentiful, the stitchers had to be more frugal. You saw less of the embroidery and more of the cross stitch, since it used less thread. Since there was more cross stitching, more variations on the stitch itself began to be used more frequently, as well as other complementary stitches.

Cross stitch landscapes made their appearances in the 18th century. They were much more detailed and realistic and could take years to complete. They were used for such things as pads for stools, furniture, and wall hangings, just to name a few. With the introduction of women's magazines and the growth of the textile industry in the 19th century, cross stitch began to be taught in school and thus became available to women from all walks of life.

In the middle of the 19th century, Berlin Wool Work caused a decline in cross stitch. The wool work designs were very popular because the colored designs were pre-printed on canvas, and then packaged with the charts and brightly colored wool used to work the designs. This made them much more accessible, with everything all together - the stitcher could get started right away and they would not have to contribute anything artistically.

Cross stitch continued to decline into the first part of the 20th century, with the advent of the sewing machines. Those who still did hand stitching tended to do embroidery - usually pre-printed designs. However, in the 1960s, counted cross stitch made a comeback, mainly with patterns for traditional samplers. The 1980s brought new patterns, more intricate stitches, and larger fabric selections; there were more thread varieties and an even stronger interest in counted cross stitch.

## *What the Guide Focuses On*

We are going to focus on counted cross stitch in this book. You will learn two different ways to start a project. You will learn about preparing material for stitching and finishing the project.

We are also going to discuss the different materials, the different types of thread, and learn some different stitches used in cross stitch embroidery.

# Chapter 1: Types of Cross Stitch

There are several different cross stitch techniques. The most commonly seen are stamped and counted.

## *Stamped Cross Stitch*

Stamped cross stitch has a pattern pre-printed on the fabric. The design appears as large X's and the color chart shows you what color to use for each section of X's. You sew over each X so that they are completely covered. The ink used to imprint the design washes out so that it is not visible once the design is finished. The X's tend to be much larger than those seen with counted cross stitch, except with the larger Aida materials.

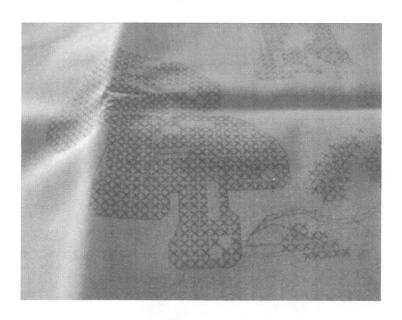

**Stamped Cross Stitch**

## *Counted Cross Stitch*

Counted cross stitch is done on plain fabric - in other words, fabric with no pattern printed on it. Instead, it comes with a pattern chart to show which stitches go where. The pattern chart is actually set up as a grid (think of graph paper) with each block on the grid representing a square on the material. The corner of each block corresponds with the holes in the fabric. The chart will either use colors or symbols to represent the different thread colors (or other items such as beads or ribbon) that will be used in the project. The legend that comes with the chart matches the symbols or colors with the thread colors.

**Counted Cross Stitch**

# Chapter 2: Materials Used for Cross Stitch

## *What You Need*

- Cross stitch (or tapestry) needles
- Embroidery floss (thread)
- Evenweave fabric (such as Aida or linen)
- Scissors (fabric and embroidery)
- Embroidery hoop or scroll frame
- Fabric Fray Check (fabric glue)

These items can be purchased at your local craft store. If you don't have one nearby, there are several large department store chains that may carry them. They can also be purchased online.

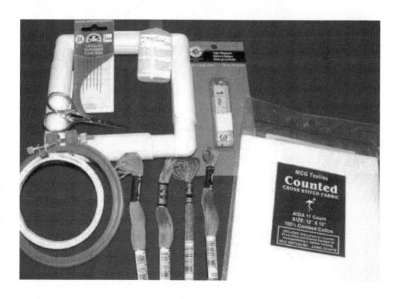

**Various Stitching Supplies**

# Chapter 3: Needles Used for Cross Stitch

Cross stitch needles, also known as tapestry needles, have rounded tips instead sharp pointed tips. The eye of these needles is also larger to make it easier to insert and hold the embroidery thread. The needles come in six different sizes and each size is used on different fabric sizes. The higher the needle number, the smaller the needle is.

**Cross Stitch Needles - Sizes 18, 20, 22**

**Cross Stitch Needles - Size 24**

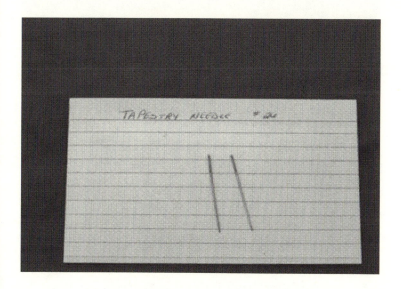

**Cross Stitch Needles - Size 26**

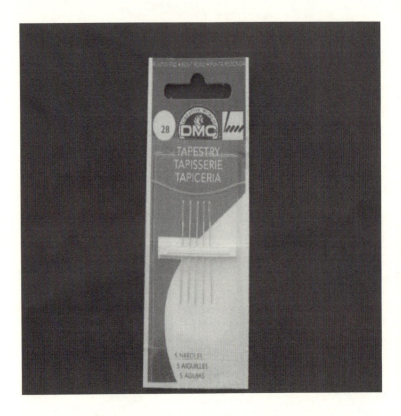

**Cross Stitch Needles - Size 28**

For the stitcher who is allergic to nickel, which is a component of most cross stitch needles, gold needles are available at a fairly reasonable price. They can also be found at the local craft stores and online.

To make it easier to figure out which needle is the best to use for which size of fabric, I've provided a list that matches needle size with fabric count size.

## *Needle Sizes Matched to Fabric Count Size*

- Size 18
    - 6-count blockweave fabrics (Aida/Binca/Herta)
- Size 20
    - 8-count blockweave (Aida/Herta)
- Size 22
    - 11-count blockweave (Aida)
    - 22-count evenweave fabrics
    - 25-count evenweave fabrics (Lugana)
    - 25-count linen fabrics (Dublin linen)
    - 27-count evenweave fabrics (Linda)
- Size 24
    - 14-count blockweave fabrics (Aida)
    - 28-count evenweave fabrics (Lugana, Jobelan)
- Size 26
    - 16-count blockweave fabrics (Aida)
    - 22-count blockweave fabrics (Hardnager/Oslo, Aida)
    - 32-count evenweave fabrics
    - 32-count linen fabrics (Belfast linen)

- Size 28
    - 18-count blockweave fabrics (Aida)
    - 36-count linen fabrics (Dublin linen)

Another type of needle that may be used by cross stitchers is the crewel embroidery needle. These needles also have large eyes to accommodate the embroidery thread, but they have sharp points. They are usually used for the non-counted cross stitch (stamped). However, some stitchers use them for half- and quarter-stitches on the Aida fabric because it makes it easier to pierce the center of the blocks for these particular stitches. There are some stitchers who use these needles to do the backstitch finishing as well.

Finally, the beading needle is used to add seed beads to your project. These needles are very slender and have small eyes. This is so that they can fit through the small openings of the glass beads.

## Beading Needles

# Chapter 4: Types of Floss Used for Cross Stitch

The selection of thread used for cross stitch is as varied as the fabric. It ranges from cotton to silk to metallic. The range of colors is unimaginable as well - deep, rich solids to light pastels to variegated threads. We will discuss those that are used most frequently.

I have provided a list below that gives the recommended number of strands per fabric count.

## *Strand Count for Cross Stitch & Backstitch for Various Fabric Counts*

- 11-count
    - Cross Stitch and specialty stitches - 3 strands
    - Backstitch - 2 strands
- 14-count, 16-count, 18-count
    - Cross Stitch and specialty stitches - 2 strands
    - Backstitch - 1 strand
- 22-count, 28-count, 32-count
    - Cross Stitch and specialty stitches - 1 strand

- Backstitch - 1 strand

    I don't always go by the recommendations. If I think the design would look better with more strands of thread in a certain area to make it stand out, then I add a few strands to that area when I'm stitching it. This only works if you aren't working from a kit, since they only furnish enough floss to finish the project with a little left over for mistakes. However, if you purchased the floss, feel free to experiment with the strand numbers to get the look you want.

    Cotton embroidery floss is used for most cross stitch projects. It usually consists of six strands of thread, which are separated in one, two, three, or four plies (strands) depending on the fabric count. However, there are some varieties that come in 3-ply, which are separated into one or two plies for projects. Another variety is a single strand available in variegated colors.

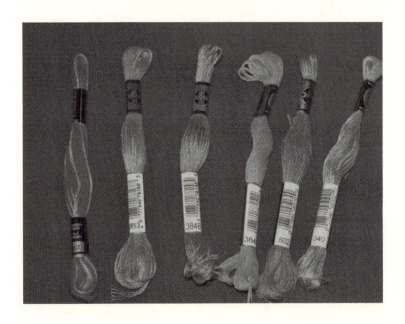

**Cotton Embroidery Floss**

Pearl cotton floss is available in variations. You have pearl cotton balls, which come in three different weights (the thread is thinner as the weight goes higher). There are pearl cotton skeins, which are a 2-ply thread that is lightly twisted together. It cannot be divided into plies and gives a raised look to your project. It is available in only one weight.

Metallic floss comes in several varieties. There is Antica which gives a soft effect. It is a heavier metallic thread that is available in antique colors. Rachelette has a very fine metallic running through the Rachel thread. It gives your projects a shimmery effect. Snow floss is an opalescent metallic thread that seems to pick up the surrounding colors around it. It can make your projects sparkle. Metallic embroidery thread also comes in a 3-ply variety that cannot be divided.

**Various Types of Metallic Threads**

There are the blend varieties. The Impressions blend is 50% wool and 50% silk, which comes only in solid colors.

Synthetic floss can be used for cross stitch as well. Rachel is a variety that looks wet and shimmery, almost transparent once it is applied to the fabric.

Silk floss can be 12-ply, in both solid and variegated colors. This floss can be separated into one ply for the fine stitches and two plies for regular cross stitches.

Linen embroidery floss is manufactured with 100% western European linen fibers. It is a 6-strand thread that can be separated in the same fashion as cotton thread for cross stitch projects.

# Chapter 5: Types of Fabrics Used for Cross Stitch

There are many different types of cloth that can be used for cross stitch, but for the best results you want to use a blockweave, an evenweave or a linen fabric. The thread count numbers tell you how many threads there are per inch in the fabric (i.e., 14-count = 14 threads in 1 inch). Fabrics over 18-count are usually stitched over 2 threads unless stated otherwise in the pattern. This technique for blockweave stitching will be demonstrated later in the book. The fabrics that are most commonly used are discussed here.

**Aida Fabric (11-count)**

## ***Aida***

Aida is a blockweave fabric. It is the fabric most commonly used for cross stitch projects, especially by those who are just starting out. It is available in a rainbow of colors, although most beginners use either the white or ivory (off white) for their first few projects because it is easier to see the holes in the fabric when making their stitches. Aida cloth is available in the following thread counts: 11, 14, 16, 18, and 22. It is also available in 6- and 8-counts, but at these counts, the fabric is called Herta or Binca.

## ***Hardnager (also known as Oslo)***

Hardnager fabric is another blockweave fabric that is available in 22-count. It can be used for both cross stitch and Hardnager embroidery. It was originally available only in white, antique white or ivory, but is now available in a much wider color selection.

**Hardnager Fabric (22-count)**

## *Anne Cloth*

Anne Cloth is one of the most popular afghan fabrics. It is used quite frequently in magazine and book patterns because it looks wonderful and it is very easy to stitch designs on it, even for beginners. Anne Cloth usually comes in a cut of 7 pattern squares wide by 9 pattern squares long. Each square gives about a 5"x5" stitching area in 14-count or 18-count. It comes in a variety of colors.

**Anne Cloth (18-count Afghan Fabric for Cross Stitch)**

## *Lady Elizabeth Afghan*

The Lady Elizabeth Afghan is another blockweave fabric that is popular for cross stitching. It usually features 14-count panels for stitching which measure approximately 6.5"x6.5". There are 20 panels to stitch on this afghan.

**Lady Elizabeth Afghan (14-count for Cross Stitch)**

## *Lugana*

Lugana is an evenweave fabric available in both 25- and 28-count, but the 25-count is the most popular. You have a nice color selection to choose from with 29 colors available. You will find that it is often the fabric of choice for patterns designed for tablecloths, cushions, and other soft furnishings.

**Lugana Fabric (25-count)**

## *Linda*

You will often find Linda cloth, which is evenweave, in the larger cross stitch kits. It is one of the more popular 27-count fabrics. Linda fabric is usually available in antique white, white, ivory, and yellow.

## *Jobelan*

Jobelan is a popular 28-count evenweave fabric used for cross stitch projects. There are at least 58 colors to choose from, depending on where you shop.

Since it is an easy-care fabric that is easy to work with, it is ideal for table linens or pillows.

## *Jubilee*

Jubilee is another evenweave fabric that is available in 28-count. Because it is 100% cotton, it is easily dyed. This makes it available in a wide range of colors.

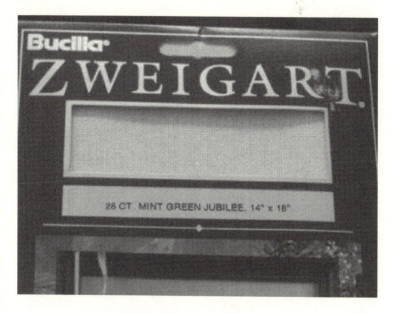

**Jubilee Fabric (28-count)**

## *Murano*

Murano is a 32-count evenweave fabric commonly used for cross stitch. You have fourteen colors to select from for your project.

## *Belfast Linen*

This 32-count fabric is the most commonly used linen for cross stitch projects. You have a wide range of colors to select from for your project. Because the threads are uneven in diameter (intentionally), it is better to save a project on this fabric for when you have a little more experience under your belt.

**Belfast Linen (32-count)**

## *Waste Canvas*

This fabric is a non-evenweave fabric used to do cross stitch on items such as shirts, bags, or jackets. It is set up as a grid so that the stitches are evenly spaced, just like cross stitch. After the project is complete, you will be able to easily separate it from the project since it is held together with water soluble glue.

**Waste Canvas (14-count)**

# Chapter 6: Types of Hoops and frames Used for Cross Stitch

There are a variety of hoops and frames used for cross stitch projects. Most stitchers choose to use them to hold the fabric taut so that the stitches are even. This keeps the fabric from puckering when stitches have different tensions. One thing you want to remember about hoops: Always, always remove your work from the hoop when you stop for the day. This is to prevent "hoop" creases in your work, which tend to stay there no matter what you do to get rid of them when you are finishing the project.

These fabric tightening tools range from frames to hoops to bars. We will briefly discuss each type here.

## *Clip-on Frames (also known as Q-Snap Frames)*

The clip-on frame is usually made of pieces of PVC pipe which are interchangeable, depending on the size of your project. You roll the fabric over the curve of the frame and clip it in place with a clip made of the same PVC material as the frame. It is very efficient in holding your material taut while you stitch. These frames come in a variety of sizes.

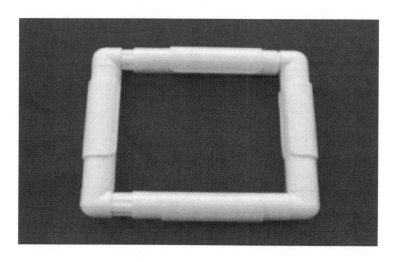

**Clip-On (Q-Snap) Frame**

## *Scroll Frames*

Scroll frames have three parts - the scroll rods, extender bars, and tightening knobs. You attach your fabric to the scroll rods. The extender bars hold the scroll bars in place as you "scroll" them up or down while you work your project. The tightening knobs are used to hold the scroll bars in place once you have them in position so that you can work your project.

There are several types of scroll bars. There is the No Basting System, which uses an application of sticky back material to the scroll rod and sticky back material to your fabric. The material attached to your fabric is permanent, so it must be cut off prior to finishing.

Another type of scroll bar system uses webbing for attaching fabric. You would sew your fabric to the webbing, thus attaching it to the scroll bar. You can do this by hand or with a sewing machine.

A similar attachment method is to tack your fabric to the scroll bar. You would use something like Japanese brass tacks for this so that there would be no discoloration from the tacks.

Finally, there is the Split Rail Scroll Rod. This is the system that I prefer since it makes it much easier to put the fabric on the scroll bar. The scroll bar is split down the middle approximately three-quarters of its length. You insert the fabric into the split, even it out, and roll it up. Another reason I like it is that I can get the fabric in the frame and get started much quicker than with any of the other scroll frame systems.

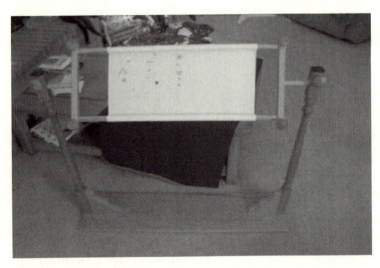

**Scroll Frame - Floor Stand**

## *Hoops*

Hoops come in a wide variety - spring tension, wood, plastic, and square or rectangle. The spring tension hoop is probably the most popular because it is the easiest to use. You place your fabric over the colorful outer hoop, and then squeeze the metal clip to fit inside the outer hoop. The metal clip fitting inside the outer ring provides the spring tension on the fabric.

The wood and plastic hoops are very similar except for the materials they are made of. They both use small screws to hold the fabric in place. The main difference is that the plastic hoop is much more durable and less likely to break after extended use.

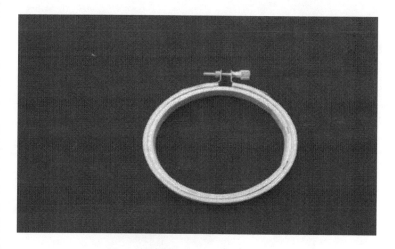

**Circular Hoop – Wooden**

**Circular Hoop - Plastic**

## *Stretcher Bars*

Stretcher bars use the same concept as stretching canvas for painting. You put the bars together to form a frame that is approximately the same size as your fabric. Then you tack your fabric to the frame using thumb tacks or a staple gun. The fabric is pulled drum tight, just like a painter's canvas.

# Chapter 7: How To prepare the fabric for a Project

If the fabric is not prepared properly it can unravel. This can cause it to become uneven and create difficulties when you start the finishing process after you complete your project. Although you will probably want to get right into working on your stitching, it is well worth it to take the time to prepare your fabric first.

## *Preparing Fabric for Stitching*

### *STEP-BY-STEP ACTION STEPS*

1. Lay your fabric out on a flat surface, preferably one that can be cleaned with alcohol after you are done.

## Preparing Fabric for Stitching - Step 1

2. Pick a corner and start applying the Fray Chek along the edges of the fabric, working your way around until you come back to the corner where you started. Take care not to apply too much since it will take longer to dry.

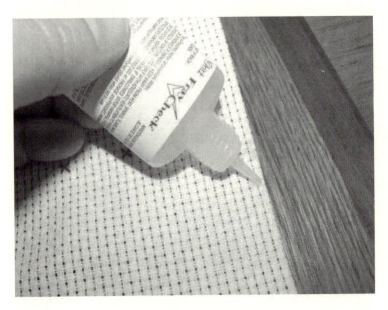

### Applying Fray Chek

3. Once you have applied the Fray Chek on all the edges, let it dry for 30 minutes before beginning to stitch.

# Chapter 8: How To find the Center Point of the Fabric

There are two methods that can be used to find the center of the fabric. This is important because this is where you want to start stitching from. If you start from the edge, you could finish the project only to find that your design is not centered on the fabric. By starting from the center of the design (and the fabric), you will be less likely to be off-center when you are finished.

## *The First METHOD - Folding*

- Fold the fabric into quarters.
- You can stick a needle in the fabric where the folds meet to mark the center point until you determine what color thread you need to make your first stitch.

### *Step-By-Step Action Steps*

1. Lay the fabric out flat.

**Finding Fabric Center (Folding Method) - Step 1**

2. Fold fabric in half lengthwise.

**Finding Fabric Center (Folding Method) - Step 2**

3. Fold fabric in half again across its width.

**Finding Fabric Center (Folding Method) - Step 3**

4. Push the needle through the fabric where the four corners of the fabric folds meet.

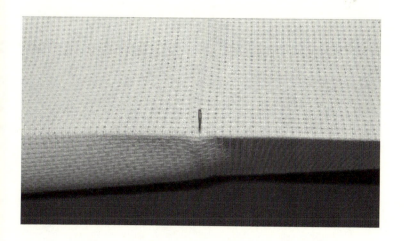

## Finding Fabric Center (Folding Method) - Step 4

5. Use a colored pushpin to mark the spot until you can get your needle threaded with the starting thread color. When placing the colored pushpin, be sure to use the colored head to mark the center point, as shown in the picture.

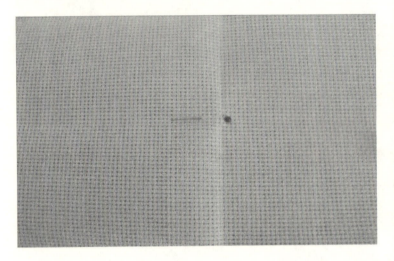

## Finding Fabric Center (Folding Method) - Step 5

## *The Second METHOD - Measuring*

- Measure the fabric down the length and divide that measurement in half to find the vertical center point (down). Then measure the fabriic across the width and divide that measurement in half to find the horizontal center point (across). The center point of the fabric is where the vertical and horizontal points meet.

## ***Step-By-Step Action Steps***

1. Lay the fabric out flat.

**Finding Fabric Center (Measurement Method) - Step 1**

2. Measure along the length of the fabric.

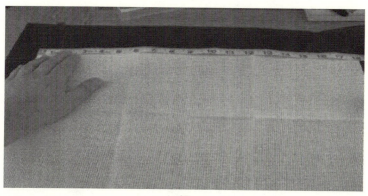

## Finding Fabric Center (Measurement Method) - Step 2

3. Mark the halfway point with a colored pushpin.

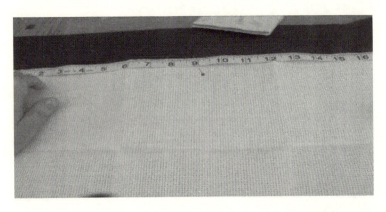

## Finding Fabric Center (Measurement Method) - Step 3

4. Measure across the width of the fabric at the colored pushpin marking the center point of the length. Mark halfway point with a colored pushpin. This is the center of the fabric.

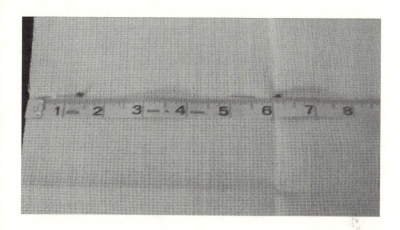

**Finding Fabric Center (Measurement Method) - Step 4**

# Chapter 9: How To Do Some of The Different Stitches of Cross Stitch

There are many different stitches used in cross stitch and many variations of the basic cross stitch as well. We would need an entire book just to demonstrate just the stitches themselves. However, since there are so many, this section will provide step-by-step instructions on those that are most commonly used.

These first steps are common for all projects. They begin the process of stitching.

## *Threading the Needle*

You will thread the needle, leaving a short tail of thread. The step-by-step directions below show you how to thread the needle using a needle threader. I find it easier to use the needle threader since the eyes on the needles can be quite small.

### *Step-By-Step Action Steps*

1. Push the thin wires of the needle threader through the eye of the needle.

**Threading the Needle - Step 1**

2. Pull one end of thread through the thin wires of the needle threader and pull it up so that it is looped over the wires of the threader.

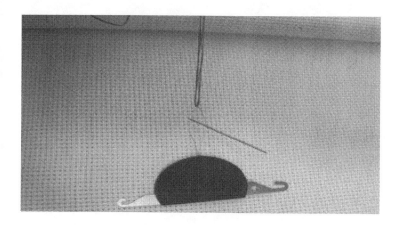

**Threading the Needle - Step 2**

3. Bring the needle up over the threader wires and thread far enough that the short thread tail you left is outside of the needle eye.

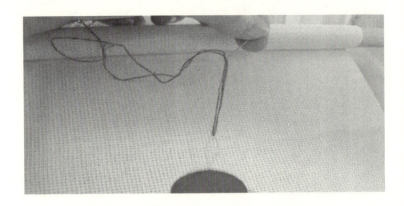

**Threading the Needle - Step 3**

4. Bring the needle up over the threader wires and thread far enough that the short thread tail you left is outside of the needle eye.

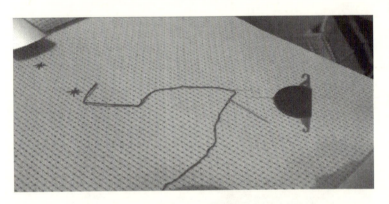

**Threading the Needle - Step 4**

5. The needle is threaded with a short tail of thread. Tie a small knot at the opposite end of the thread.

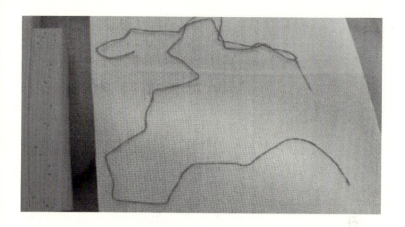

**Threaded Needle with Knot at Opposite End**

Now we will start learning how to do some of the stitches that used most frequently in cross stitch projects.

**TIP 1:** To finish threads, you will push the threaded needle under the completed stitches on the back of the fabric.

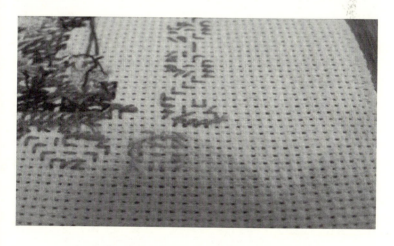

**Finished Thread (Back of Fabric)**

**TIP 2:** You want to avoid taking your thread across long distances on your design. If you come to a point in your pattern that requires you to skip over a large space (I would say no more than three or four), then you will want to anchor your thread as mentioned in Tip 1 above. This will give your work a more finished look and will keep the colors of the thread from showing through the fabric in your finished project (especially if you are using bright colored thread with the lighter fabrics).

**TIP 3:** Do not turn your fabric as you stitch (unless your pattern specifically tells you to. You want all of your stitches to face in the same direction. Again, it gives your project a more finished look.

## *Cross Stitch (also known as the English Cross stitch or sampler stitch)*

- This is the basic stitch of cross stitch projects.

### *Step-By-Step Action Steps*

1. Bring the needle up to the front of the fabric at the top left corner of the block.

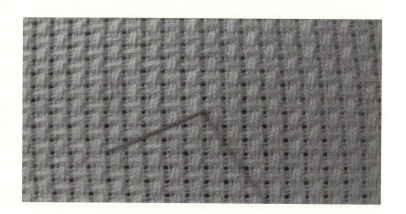

**Cross Stitch - Step 1**

2. Bring the needle across the block diagonally to push it down through the fabric at the bottom right corner of the block.

**Cross Stitch - Step 2**

3. Bring the needle up to the front of the fabric at the bottom left corner of the block.

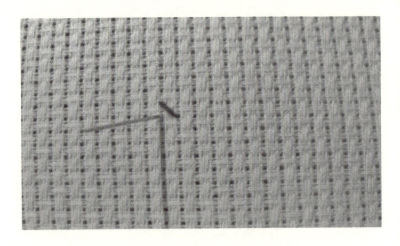

**Cross Stitch - Step 3**

4. Bring the needle across the block diagonally to push it down through the fabric at the top right corner of the block.

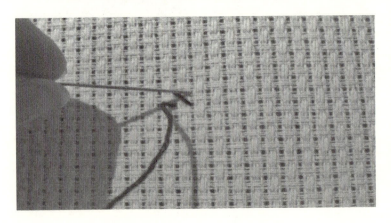

**Cross Stitch - Step 4**

5. The cross stitch is complete. Repeat the steps above as required for the pattern you are sewing.

**Cross Stitch – Completed**

## *Quarter-Cross Stitch*

- This stitch is used to fill in space that would otherwise be blocky or to separate colors in your pattern.

### *Step-By-Step Action Steps*

1. Bring the needle up to the front of the fabric at the bottom left corner of the block.

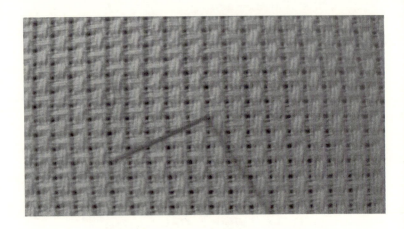

**Quarter Cross Stitch - Step 1**

2. Bring the needle across the block diagonally to push it down through the fabric at the center of the block.

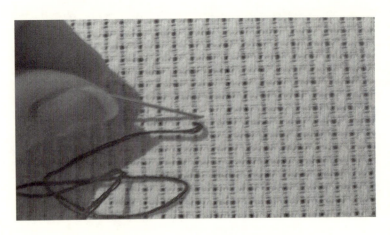

**Quarter Cross Stitch - Step 2**

3. The quarter cross stitch is complete. Repeat as needed for the pattern you are working.

**Quarter Cross Stitch - Completed**

The steps above will work to make a quarter cross stitch from any direction within the block on the material. You will just start from the corner noted on your pattern.

## *Three-Quarter Cross Stitch*

- This stitch is also used to fill in space that would otherwise be blocky or to separate colors in your pattern.

### *Step-By-Step Action Steps*

1. Bring the needle up to the front of the fabric at the top left corner of the block.

**Three-Quarter Cross Stitch - Step 1**

2. Bring the needle across the block diagonally to push it down through the fabric at the bottom right corner of the block.

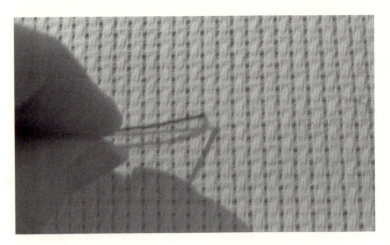

**Three-Quarter Cross Stitch - Step 2**

3. Bring the needle up to the front of the fabric at the bottom left corner of the block.

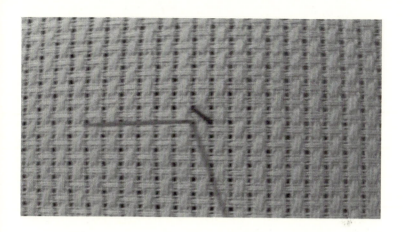

**Three-Quarter Cross Stitch - Step 3**

4. Bring the needle across the block diagonally to push it down through the fabric at the center of the block. The three-quarter cross stitch is complete. Repeat as needed for the pattern you are working.

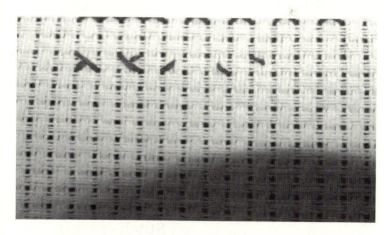

**Three-Quarter Cross Stitch - Step 4**

The steps above will work to make a three-quarter cross stitch from any direction within the block on the material. You will just start from the corner noted on your pattern, as shown in the picture above.

## *Backstitch*

- This stitch is used to provide finishing detail.

### *Step-By-Step Action Steps*

1. Bring the needle up to the front of the fabric at the left corner of the block. Your pattern will indicate whether you will be starting at the top of the block or the bottom; on the right or the left. For this demonstration, we will assume the pattern is a straight line across the bottom of four blocks in a pattern.

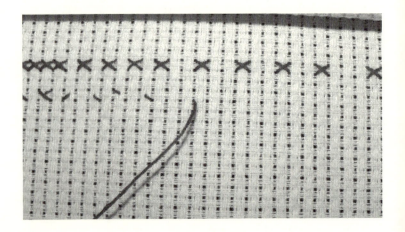

## Backstitch - Step 1

2. Bring the needle straight across the block to push it down through the fabric at the bottom right corner of the block.

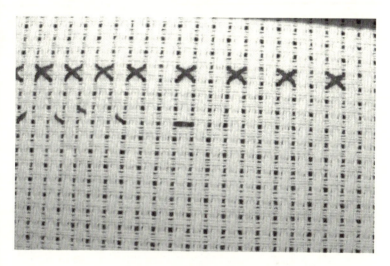

## Backstitch - Step 2

3. Bring the needle up to the front of the fabric at the bottom right corner of the next block. The reason we moved across the block is to keep from pulling the thread back out of the stitch we just completed in Step 2.

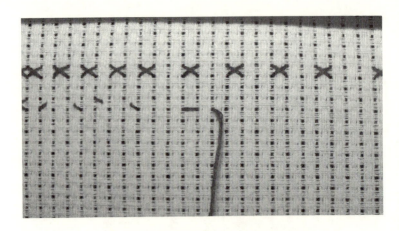

**Backstitch - Step 3**

4. Bring the needle back across the block to push it down through the fabric at the bottom left corner of the current block.

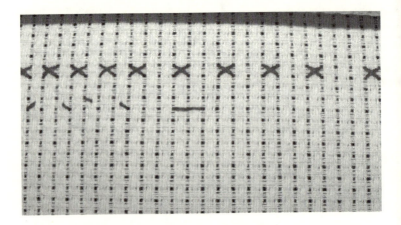

**Backstitch - Step 4**

5. Bring the needle up to the front of the fabric at the bottom left corner of the next block. We can come up in the left corner of this block

because we took the last stitch down in the left corner of the last block. We won't be pulling the stitch out that we did in Step 4.

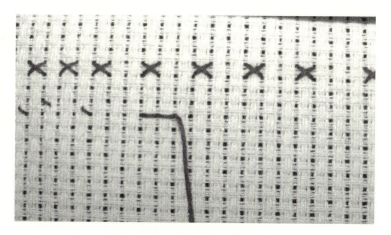

**Backstitch - Step 5**

6. Bring the needle back across the block to push it down through the fabric at the bottom right corner of the current block.

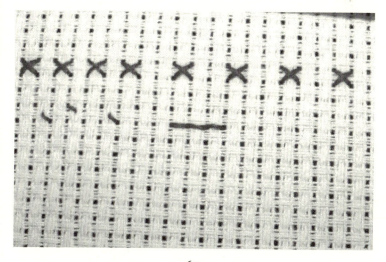

## Backstitch - Step 6

7. Bring the needle up to the front of the fabric at the bottom right corner of the next block. Once again we moved across the block to keep from pulling the thread back out of the stitch we just completed in Step 6.

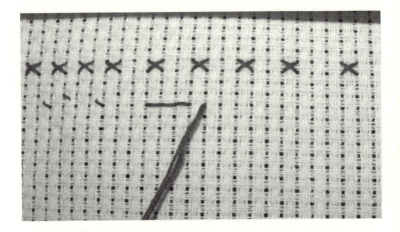

## Backstitch - Step 7

8. Bring the needle back across the block to push it down through the fabric at the bottom left corner of the current block.

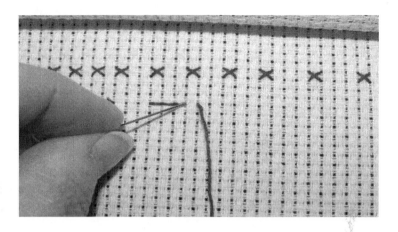

**Backstitch - Step 8**

9. The backstitch is complete (for this example).

**Backstitch - Completed**

# *Herringbone Stitch*

- This stitch is often used in samplers to divide rows or patterns in the project. It gives a nice geometric look to your project.

## ***Step-By-Step Action Steps***

1. Bring the needle up to the front of the fabric at the top left corner of the block.

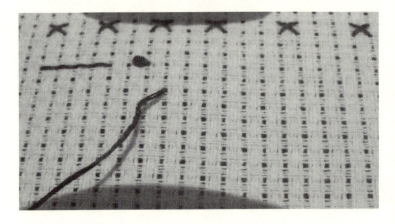

**Herringbone Stitch - Step 1**

2. Count down one block and over two blocks to the right. Push the needle down through the fabric at the bottom right corner of the second block.

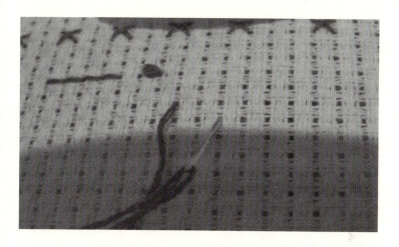

**Herringbone Stitch - Step 2**

3. Count over two blocks to the left. Bring the needle up to the front of the fabric at the bottom left corner of the second block.

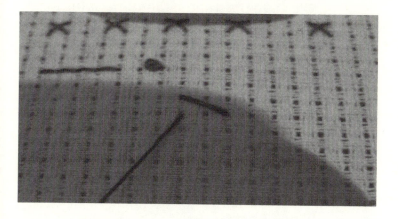

**Herringbone Stitch - Step 3**

4. Count over four blocks to the right and up two blocks. Push the needle down through the

fabric at the top right corner of the second block.

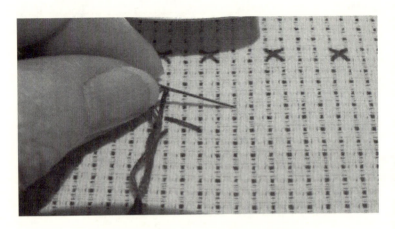

**Herringbone Stitch - Step 4**

5. Count over two blocks to the left. Bring the needle up to the front of the fabric at the top left corner of the second block.

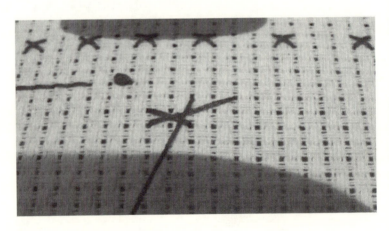

**Herringbone Stitch - Step 5**

6. Count over four blocks to the right and down two blocks. Push the needle down through the fabric at the bottom right corner of the second block.

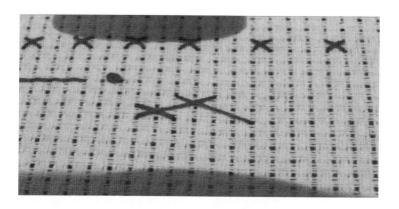

**Herringbone Stitch - Step 6**

7. Count over two blocks to the left. Bring the needle up to the front of the fabric at the bottom left corner of the second block.

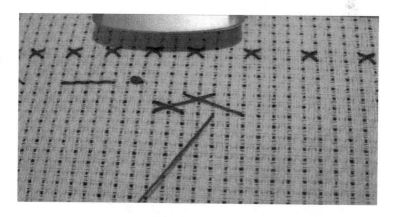

**Herringbone Stitch - Step 7**

8. Count over four blocks to the right and up two blocks. Push the needle down through the fabric at the top right corner of the second block.

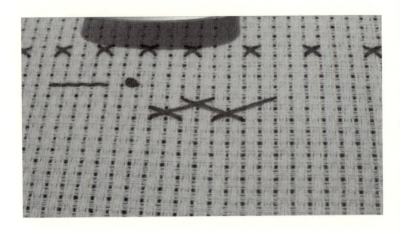

**Herringbone Stitch - Step 8 (Completed)**

9. The Herringbone Stitch is completed.

# *Long Stitch/Short Stitch (also known as the Brick stitch)*

- This stitch is used to provide shading effects when blending colors.

## *Step-By-Step Action Steps*

1. Bring the needle up to the front of the fabric at the top left corner of the block.

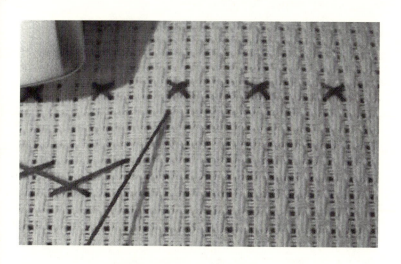

**Long Stitch/Short Stitch - Step 1**

2. Bring the needle straight down two blocks to push it down through the fabric at the bottom left corner of the second block. This is the Short Stitch.

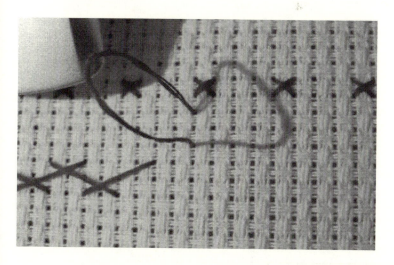

**Long Stitch/Short Stitch - Step 2**

3. Count over one block and up two blocks. Bring the needle up to the front of the fabric at the top right corner of the second block.

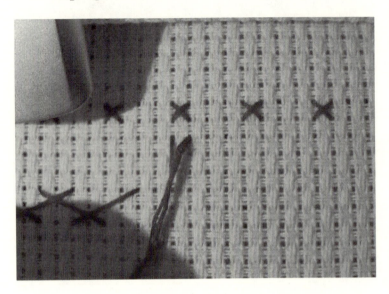

**Long Stitch/Short Stitch - Step 3**

4. Bring the needle straight down the three blocks to push it down through the fabric at the bottom right corner of the third block. This is the Long Stitch.

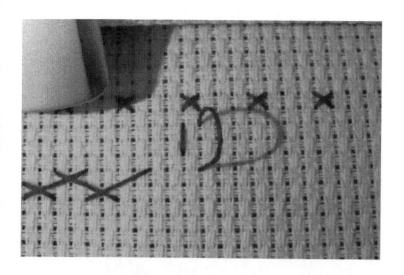

## Long Stitch/Short Stitch - Step 4

5. Count over one block and up three blocks. Bring the needle up to the front of the fabric at the top right corner of the third block.

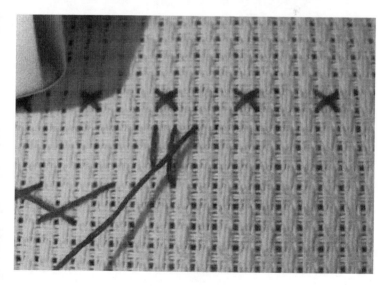

## Long Stitch/Short Stitch - Step 5

6. Bring the needle straight down two blocks to push it down through the fabric at the bottom left corner of the second block. This makes another Short Stitch.

## Long Stitch/Short Stitch - Step 6

7. Count over one block and up two blocks. Bring the needle up to the front of the fabric at the top right corner of the second block.

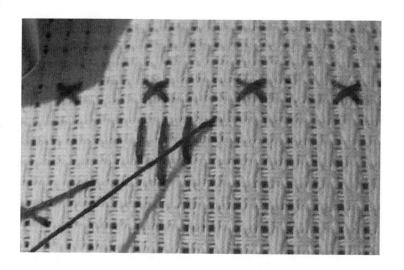

**Long Stitch/Short Stitch - Step 7**

8. Bring the needle straight down the three blocks to push it down through the fabric at the bottom right corner of the third block. This makes another Long Stitch.

**Long Stitch/Short Stitch - Step 8**

9. Long Stitch/Short Stitch is completed.

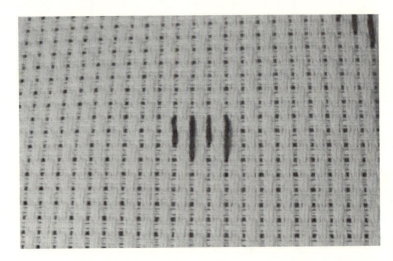

**Long Stitch/Short Stitch - Completed**

## *Double Cross Stitch*

- This stitch is used as a border or to outline a design. It can also be used as filler for a design. It looks almost exactly like the Smyrna Cross Stitch, but the bottom layer looks like a plus sign and the top layer looks the cross stitch.

### ***Step-By-Step Action Steps***

1. Bring the needle up to the front of the fabric at the left corner of the block.

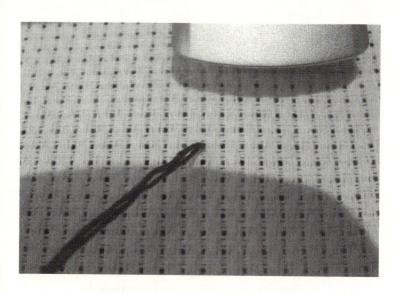

**Double Cross Stitch - Step 1**

2. Bring the needle straight across two blocks to push the needle down through the fabric at the center right corner.

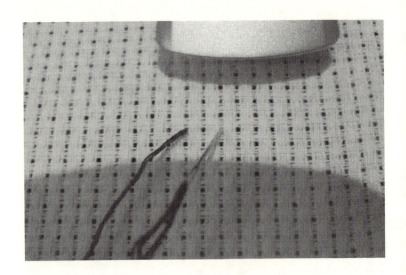

## Double Cross Stitch - Step 2

3. Count up one block and over to the left one block from where you pushed the needle down through the fabric in Step 2. Bring the needle up to the front of the fabric in the top left corner.

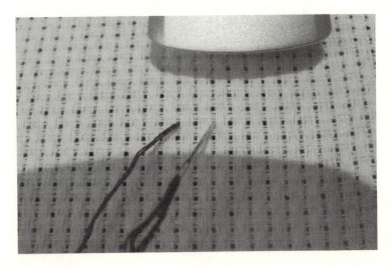

## Double Cross Stitch - Step 3

4. Bring the needle straight down across two blocks to push the needle down through the fabric at the bottom left hole.

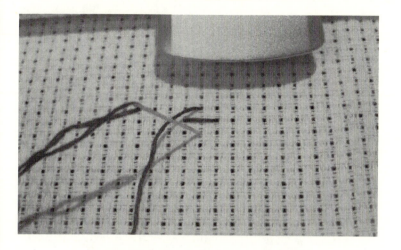

## Double Cross Stitch - Step 4

5. Count two blocks over to the left and two blocks up from where you pushed the needle down through the fabric in Step 4. Bring the needle up through the fabric in the top left corner of the block.

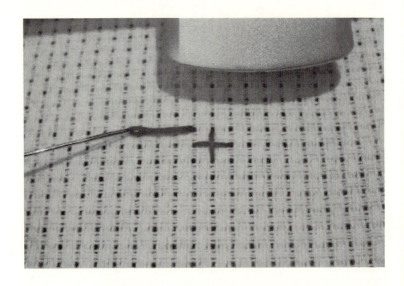

**Double Cross Stitch - Step 5**

6. Bring the needle diagonally down across the entire stitch to push the needle down through the fabric at the bottom right corner of the second block.

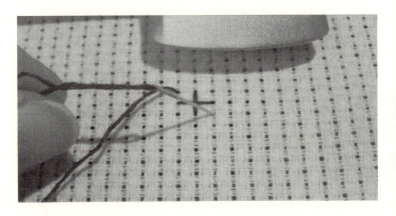

**Double Cross Stitch - Step 6**

7. Count two blocks over to the left from where you pushed the needle down through the fabric in Step 6. Bring the needle up to the front of the fabric at the bottom left corner.

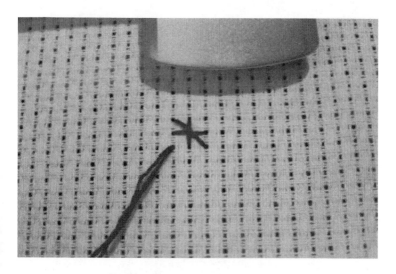

**Double Cross Stitch - Step 7**

8. Bring the needle diagonally across the entire stitch to push the needle down through the fabric at the top right corner of the second block.

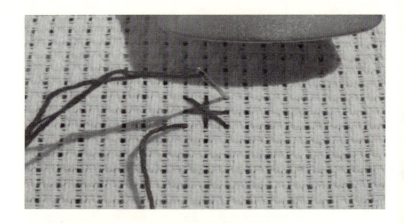

**Double Cross Stitch - Step 8**

9. The Double Cross Stitch is complete.

**Double Cross Stitch – Completed**

## *Smyrna Cross Stitch*

- This stitch is also used as a border, to outline a design, or as filler for a design. It looks almost exactly like the Double Cross Stitch, but the bottom layer looks like a cross stitch and the top layer looks like a plus sign.

### *Step-By-Step Action Steps*

1. Bring the needle up to the front of the fabric at the top left corner of the block.

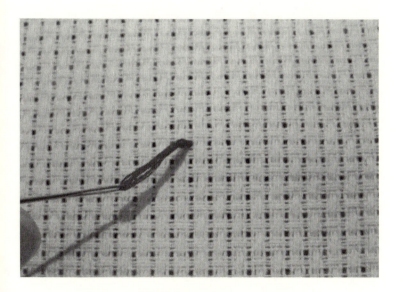

**Smyrna Cross Stitch - Step 1**

2. Count two blocks over and two blocks down from where you brought the needle up to the front of the fabric in Step 1. Bring the needle

across the block diagonally to push it down
through the fabric at the bottom right corner of
the second block down and across.

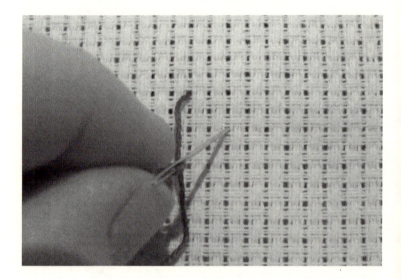

**Smyrna Cross Stitch - Step 2**

3. Count two blocks over to the left from where
you pushed the needle down through the fabric
in Step 2. Bring the needle up to the front of
the fabric at the bottom left corner of the
second block.

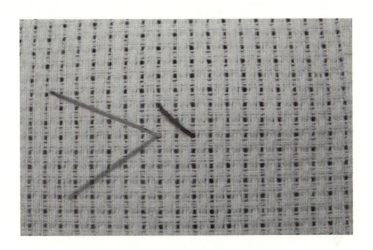

**Smyrna Cross Stitch - Step 3**

4. Count two blocks over to the left and two block up from where you brought the needle up to the front of the fabric in Step 3. Bring the needle across the block diagonally to push it down through the fabric at the top right corner of the block.

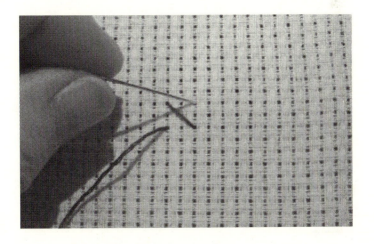

**Smyrna Cross Stitch - Step 4**

5. Count two blocks over to the left and one block down from where you pushed the needle down through the fabric in Step 4. Bring the needle up to the front of the fabric at the center left corner.

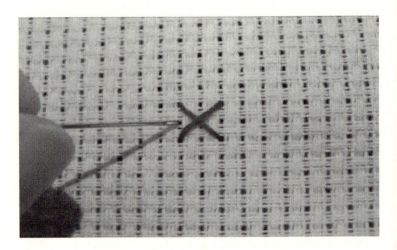

**Smyrna Cross Stitch - Step 5**

6. Bring the needle straight across the cross stitch to push the needle down through the fabric at the center right corner.

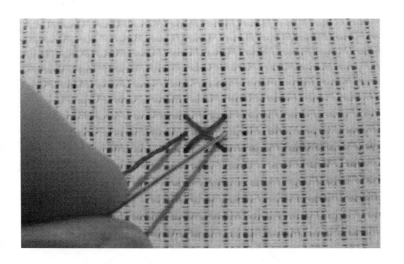

**Smyrna Cross Stitch - Step 6**

7. Count up one block and over to the left one block from where you pushed the needle down through the fabric in Step 6. Bring the needle up to the front of the fabric at the top center hole.

**Smyrna Cross Stitch - Step 7**

8. Bring the needle straight down across the entire stitch to push the needle down through the fabric at the center bottom hole.

**Smyrna Cross Stitch - Step 8**

9. The Smyrna Cross Stitch is complete.

**Smyrna Cross Stitch - Completed**

## *Four-sided Stitch*

- This stitch is most commonly used as a border or to outline a design.

### *Step-By-Step Action Steps*

1. Bring the needle up to the front of the fabric at the top left corner of the block.

**Four-sided Stitch - Step 1**

2. Bring the needle down two blocks and push the needle down through the fabric at the bottom left corner of the second block.

**Four-Sided Stitch - Step 2**

3. Count two blocks to the right and up two blocks. Bring the needle up to the front of the fabric at the top right corner of the second block.

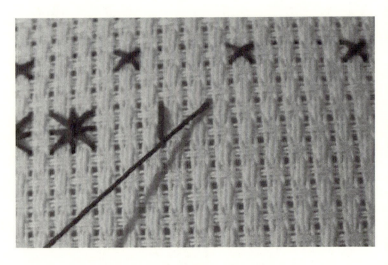

**Four-Sided Stitch - Step 3**

4. Bring the needle straight across two blocks to the left to push the needle down through the fabric at the top left corner of the second block. This should be the block where you originally came up to start the first part of the stitch.

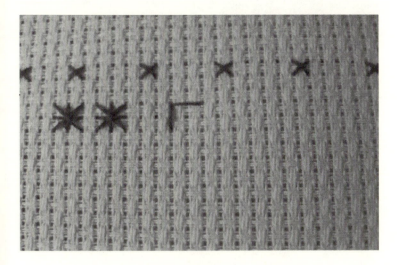

**Four-Sided Stitch - Step 4**

5. Count two blocks to the right and down two blocks. Bring the needle up to the front of the fabric at the bottom right corner of the second block.

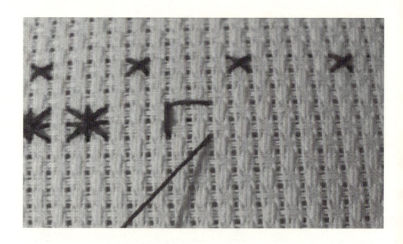

**Four-Sided Stitch - Step 5**

6. Bring the needle straight across two blocks to the left to push the needle down through the fabric at the bottom left corner of the second block.

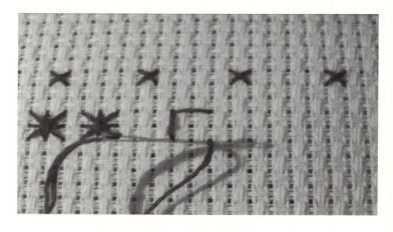

**Four-Sided Stitch - Step 6**

7. Count two blocks to the right and up two blocks. Bring the needle up to the front of the

fabric at the top right corner of the second block.

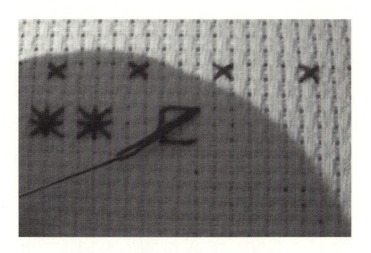

**Four-Sided Stitch - Step 7**

8. Bring the needle down two blocks and push it down through the fabric at the bottom right corner of the second block.

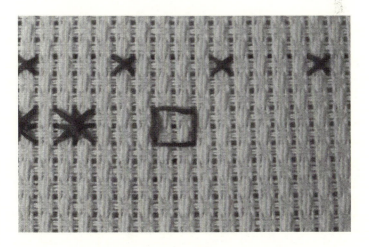

**Four-Sided Stitch - Step 8**

9. Count two blocks to the right and up two blocks. Bring the needle up to the front of the fabric at the top right corner of the second block.

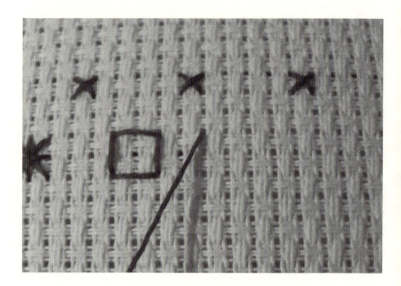

**Four-Sided Stitch - Step 9**

10. Bring the needle straight across two blocks to the left to push it down through the fabric at the top left corner of the second block.

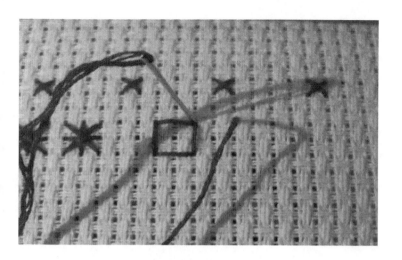

**Four-Sided Stitch - Step 10**

11. Count two blocks to the right and down two blocks. Bring the needle up to the front of the fabric at the bottom right corner of the second block.

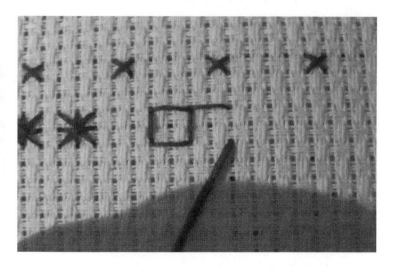

**Four-Sided Stitch - Step 11**

12. Bring the needle straight across two blocks to the right to push it down through the fabric at the bottom left corner of the second block.

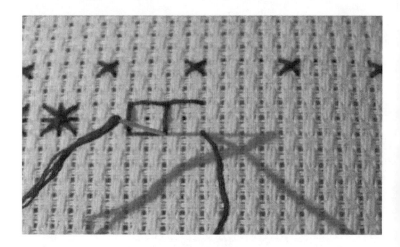

**Four-Sided Stitch - Step 12**

13. Count two blocks to the right and up two blocks. Bring the needle up to the front of the fabric at the top right corner of the second block.

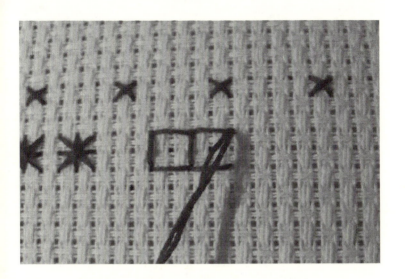

**Four-Sided Stitch - Step 13**

14. Bring the needle straight down two blocks and push it down through the fabric at the bottom right corner of the second block.

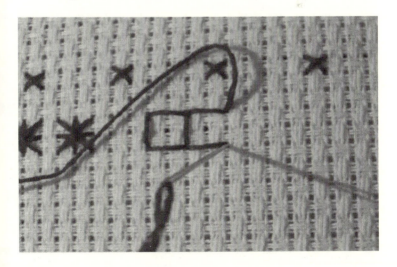

**Four-Sided Stitch - Step 14**

15. The Four-Sided Stitch is completed.

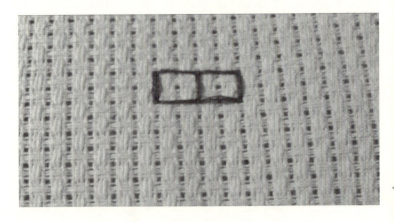

**Four-Sided Stitch - Completed**

## *Hungarian Stitch*

- This stitch is used for geometric designs or as a background stitch.

### *Step-By-Step Action Steps*

1. Bring the needle up to the front of the fabric at the bottom left corner of the block.

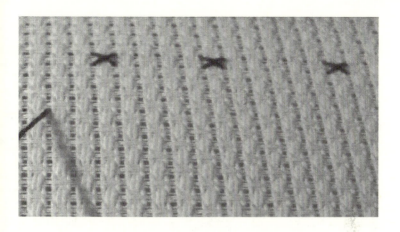

**Hungarian Stitch - Step 1**

2. Bring the needle straight up two blocks and push the needle down through the fabric at the top left corner of the second block.

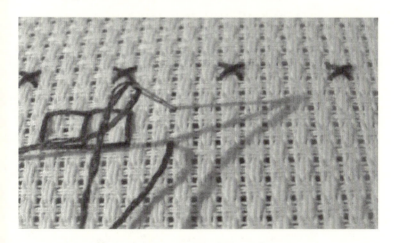

**Hungarian Stitch - Step 2**

3. Count over one block and down three blocks. Bring the needle up the front of the fabric at the bottom right corner of the third block.

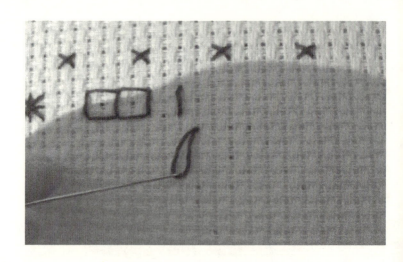

**Hungarian Stitch - Step 3**

4. Bring the needle straight up four blocks to push the needle down through the fabric at the top right corner of the fourth block.

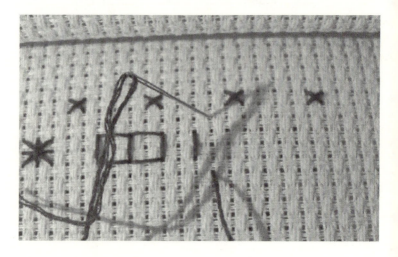

**Hungarian Stitch - Step 4**

5. Count one block to the right and down three blocks. Bring the needle to the front of the fabric at the bottom right corner of the third block.

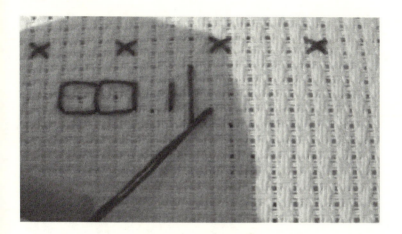

**Hungarian Stitch - Step 5**

6. Bring the needle straight up two blocks and push it down through the fabric at the top right corner of the second block.

**Hungarian Stitch - Step 6**

7. The Hungarian Stitch is completed.

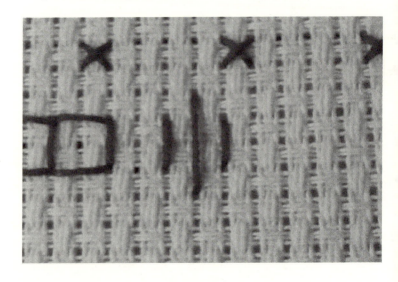

**Hungarian Stitch – Completed**

## *Algerian Eye Stitch*

- This stitch is used as a decorative stitch to provide a lacy look to your project.

### *Step-By-Step Action Steps*

1. Bring the needle up to the front of the fabric at the top left corner of the block.

**Algerian Eye Stitch - Step 1**

2. Bring the needle straight down three blocks and push it down through the fabric at the bottom left corner of the third block.

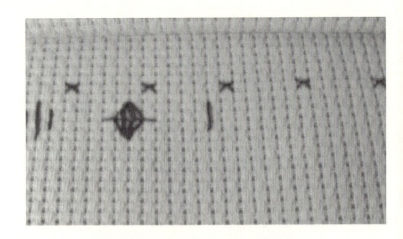

**Algerian Eye Stitch - Step 2**

3. Count three blocks over to the right and up three blocks. Bring the needle up through the fabric at the top right corner of the third block.

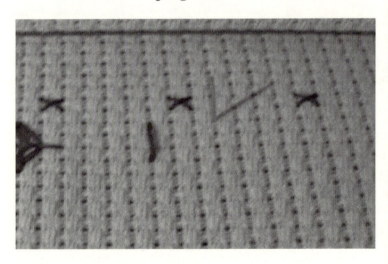

**Algerian Eye Stitch - Step 3**

4. Count three blocks down and three blocks to the left. Push the needle down through the fabric at the bottom right corner of the third block.

**Algerian Eye Stitch - Step 4**

5. Count three blocks down and three blocks to the left. Push the needle down through the fabric at the bottom right corner of the third block.

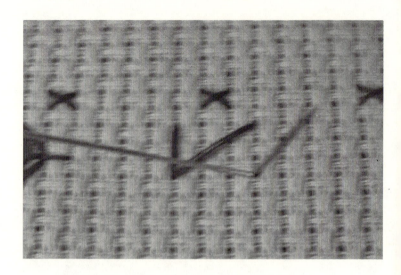

**Algerian Eye Stitch - Step 5**

6. Count three blocks to the right. Bring the fabric up to the front of the fabric at the bottom right corner of the third block.

**Algerian Eye Stitch - Step 6**

7. Count three blocks down and three blocks to the left. Push the needle down through the fabric at the bottom right corner of the third block.

**Algerian Eye Stitch - Step 7**

8. Count three blocks to the left and three blocks up. Push the needle down through the fabric at the top left corner of the third block.

**Algerian Eye Stitch - Step 8**

9. Count three blocks straight down. Bring the needle up to the front of the fabric at the bottom left corner of the third block.

**Algerian Eye Stitch - Step 9**

10. Count three blocks straight up. Push the needle down through the fabric at the top left corner of the third block.

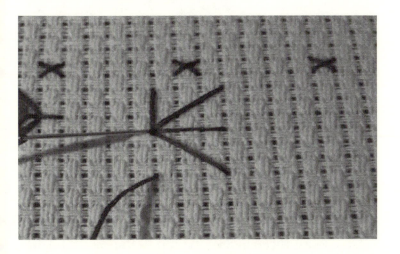

**Algerian Eye Stitch - Step 10**

11. Count three blocks to the left. Bring the needle up to the front of the fabric at the bottom left corner of the third block.

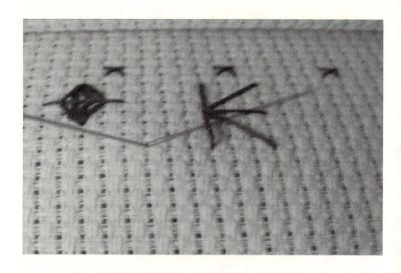

**Algerian Eye Stitch - Step 11**

12. Count three blocks up and to the right. Push the needle through the fabric at the top right corner of the third block.

**Algerian Eye Stitch – Step 12**

13. Count three blocks to the left. Bring the needle up to the front of the fabric at the top left corner of the third block.

**Algerian Eye Stitch – Step 13**

14. Count three blocks to the right. Push the needle down through the fabric at the top right corner of the third block.

**Algerian Eye Stitch – Step 14**

15. Count three blocks up and three blocks to the left. Bring the needle up to the front of the fabric at the top left corner of the third block.

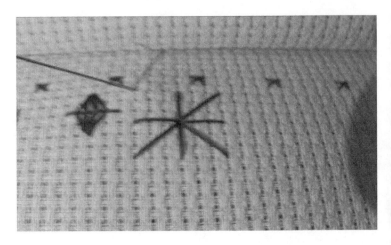

**Algerian Eye Stitch – Step 15**

16. Count three blocks to the right and three blocks down. Push the needle down through the fabric at the bottom right corner of the third block.

**Algerian Eye Stitch – Step 16**

17. The Algerian Eye Stitch is completed.

**Algerian Eye Stitch - Completed**

## *Eyelet Stitch*

- This stitch is used as a filler stitch and looks like the Algerian Eye Stitch with extra legs.

### *Step-By-Step Action Steps*

1. Bring the needle up to the front of the fabric at the top left corner of the block.

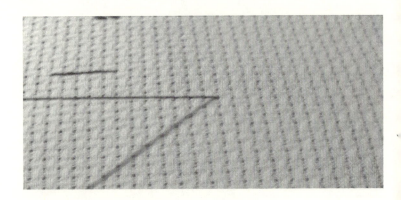

**Eyelet Stitch – Step 1**

2. Count down two blocks and push the needle through the fabric at the bottom left corner of the second block.

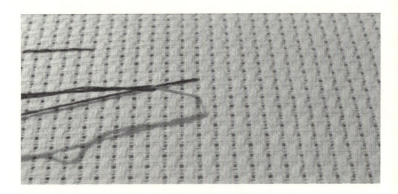

**Eyelet Stitch – Step 2**

3. Count one block to the right and two blocks up. Bring the needle up to the front of the fabric at the top right corner of the second block.

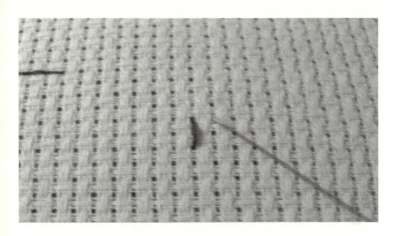

**Eyelet Stitch – Step 3**

4. Count down two blocks and one block to the left. Push the needle down through the fabric at the bottom left corner of the block.

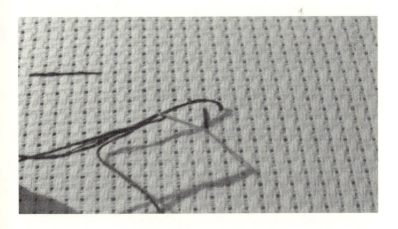

**Eyelet Stitch – Step 4**

5. Count two blocks to the right and two blocks up. Bring the needle up to the front of the fabric at the top right corner of the second block.

**Eyelet Stitch – Step 5**

6. Count two blocks down and two blocks to the left. Push the needle down through the fabric at the bottom left corner of the second block.

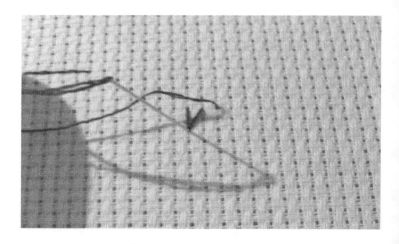

**Eyelet Stitch – Step 6**

7. Count two blocks to the right and one block up. Bring the needle up to the front of the fabric at the top right corner of the block.

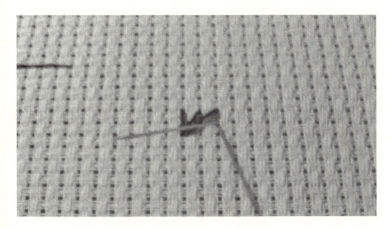

**Eyelet Stitch – Step 7**

8. Count one block down and two blocks to the left. Push the needle down through the fabric at the bottom left corner of the second block.

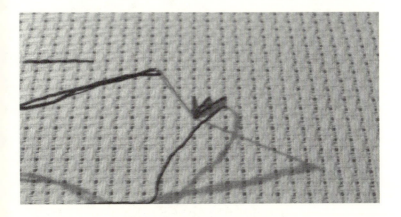

**Eyelet Stitch – Step 8**

9. Count two blocks to the right. Bring the needle up to the front of the fabric at the bottom right corner of the second block.

**Eyelet Stitch – Step 9**

10. Count two blocks to the left. Push the needle down through the fabric at the bottom left corner of the second block.

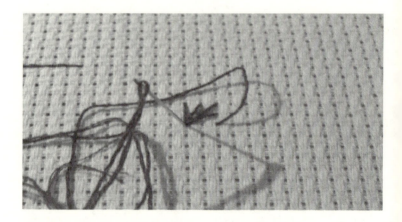

**Eyelet Stitch – Step 10**

11. Count one block down and two blocks to the right. Bring the needle up to the front of the fabric at the bottom right corner of the second block.

**Eyelet Stitch – Step 11**

12. Count two blocks to the left and one block up. Push the needle down through the fabric at the top left corner of the block.

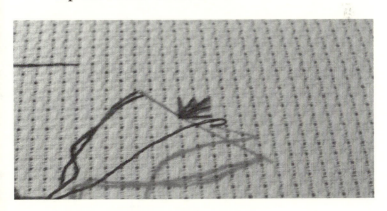

**Eyelet Stitch – Step 12**

13. Count two blocks down and two blocks to the right. Bring the needle up to the front of the fabric at the bottom right corner of the second block.

**Eyelet Stitch – Step 13**

14. Count two blocks to the left and two blocks up. Push the needle through the fabric at the top left corner of the second block.

**Eyelet Stitch – Step 14**

15. Count two blocks down and one block to the right. Bring the needle up to the front of the fabric at the bottom left corner of the block.

**Eyelet Stitch – Step 15**

16. Count one block to the left and two blocks up. Push the needle down through the fabric at the top left corner of the second block.

**Eyelet Stitch – Step 16**

17. Count two blocks down. Bring the needle up to the front of the fabric at the bottom left corner of the second block.

**Eyelet Stitch – Step 17**

18. Count two blocks up. Push the needle down through the fabric at the top left corner of the second block.

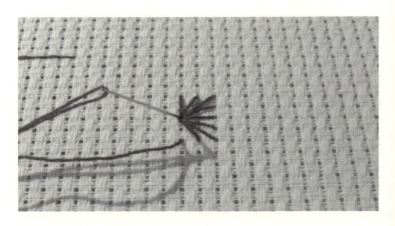

**Eyelet Stitch – Step 18**

19. Count one block to the left and two blocks down. Bring the needle up to the front of the fabric at the bottom left corner of the second block.

**Eyelet Stitch – Step 19**

20. Count two blocks up and one block to the right. Push the needle down through the fabric at the top right corner of the block.

**Eyelet Stitch – Step 20**

21. Count two blocks to the left and two blocks down. Bring the needle up to the front of the fabric at the bottom left corner of the second block.

**Eyelet Stitch – Step 21**

22. Count two blocks up and two blocks to the right. Push the needle down through the fabric at the top right corner of the second block.

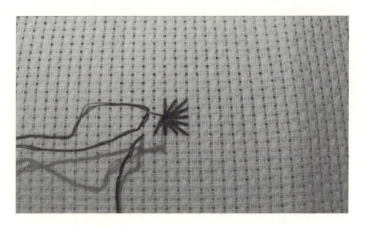

**Eyelet Stitch – Step 22**

23. Count two blocks to the left and one block down. Bring the needle up to the front of the fabric at the bottom left corner of the block.

**Eyelet Stitch – Step 23**

24. Count one block up and two blocks to the right. Push the needle down through the fabric at the top right corner of the second block.

**Eyelet Stitch – Step 24**

25. Count two blocks to the left. Bring the needle up to the front of the fabric at the bottom left corner of the block.

**Eyelet Stitch – Step 25**

26. Count two blocks to the right. Push the needle down through the fabric at the bottom right corner of the block.

**Eyelet Stitch – Step 26**

27. Count one block up and two blocks to the left. Bring the needle up to the front of the fabric at the top left corner of the second block.

**Eyelet Stitch – Step 27**

28. Count two blocks to the right and one block down. Push the needle down through the fabric at the bottom right corner of the block.

**Eyelet Stitch – Step 28**

29. Count two blocks up and two blocks to the left. Bring the needle up to the front of the fabric at the top left corner of the second block.

**Eyelet Stitch – Step 29**

30. Count two blocks to the right and two blocks down. Push the needle down through the fabric at the bottom right corner of the second block.

**Eyelet Stitch – Step 30**

31. Count two blocks up and one block to the left. Bring the needle up to the front of the fabric at the top left corner of the block.

**Eyelet Stitch – Step 31**

32. Count one block to the right and two blocks down. Push the needle down through the fabric at the bottom right corner of the second block.

**Eyelet Stitch – Step 32**

33. The Eyelet Stitch is completed.

**Eyelet Stitch – Completed**

# *Tent Stitch*

- This stitch is also known as the Basketweave Stitch when worked on the diagonal. It is used to almost as frequently as the Cross Stitch since it provides the same coverage.

## *Step-By-Step Action Steps*

1. Bring the needle up to the front of the fabric at the top left corner of the block.

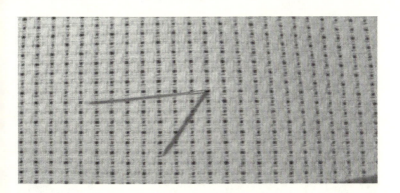

**Tent Stitch – Step 1**

2. Cross the block diagonally to the left. Push the needle down through the fabric at the top right corner of the block.

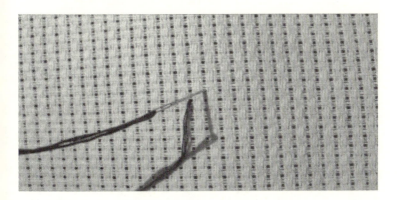

**Tent Stitch – Step 2**

3. Count two blocks to the left and one block down. Bring the needle up to the front of the fabric at the bottom left corner of the block.

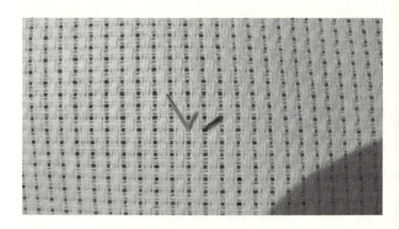

**Tent Stitch – Step 3**

4. Count one block up and one block to the right. Push the needle down through the fabric at the top right corner of the block.

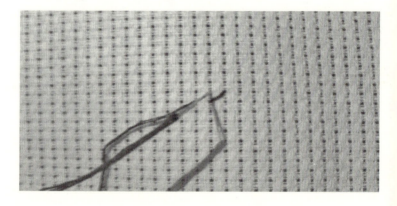

**Tent Stitch – Step 4**

5. Count two blocks to the left and one block down. Bring the needle up to the front of the fabric at the bottom left corner of the block.

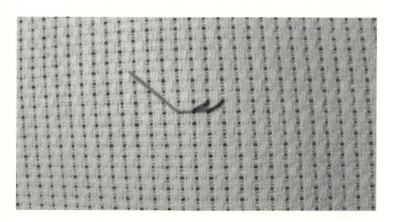

**Tent Stitch – Step 5**

6. Count one block up and one block to the right. Push the needle down through the fabric at the top right corner of the block.

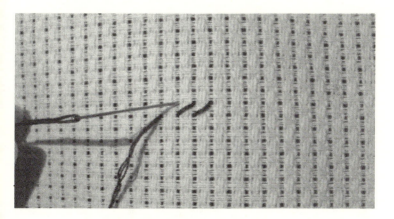

**Tent Stitch – Step 6**

7. Count two blocks to the left and one block down. Bring the needle up to the front of the fabric at the bottom left corner of the block.

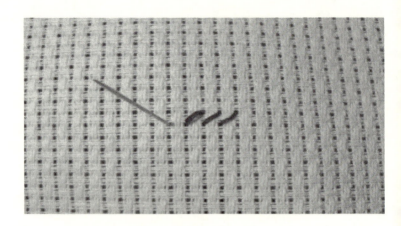

**Tent Stitch – Step 7**

8. Count one up and one block to the right. Push the needle down through the fabric at the top right corner of the block.

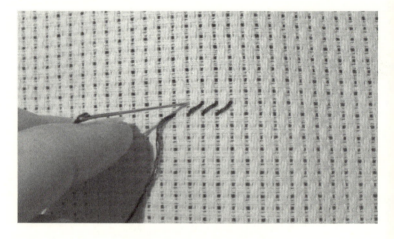

**Tent Stitch – Step 8**

9. Count one block down. Bring the needle up to the front of the fabric at the bottom right corner of the block.

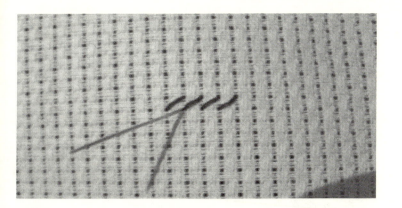

**Tent Stitch – Step 9**

10. Count one block down. Push the needle down through the fabric at the bottom left corner of the block.

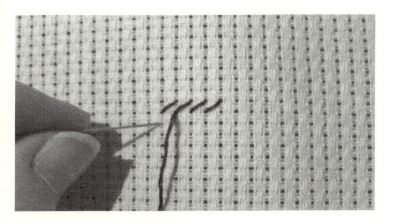

**Tent Stitch – Step 10**

11. Count two blocks to the right. Bring the needle up to the front of the fabric at the top right corner of the block.

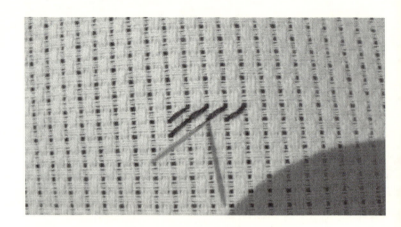

**Tent Stitch – Step 11**

12. Count one block down and one block to the left. Push the needle down through the fabric at the bottom left corner of the block.

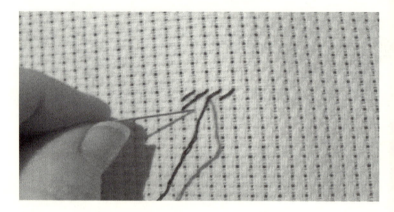

**Tent Stitch – Step 12**

13. Count two blocks to the right and one block up. Bring the needle up to the front of the fabric at the top right corner of the block.

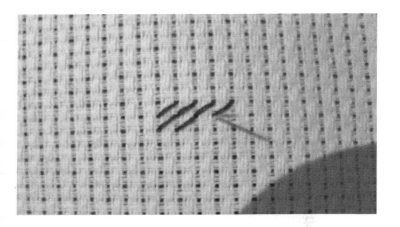

**Tent Stitch – Step 13**

14. Count one block down and one block to the left. Push the needle down through the fabric at the bottom left corner of the block.

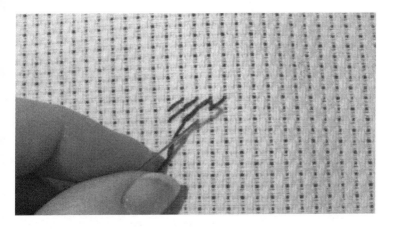

**Tent Stitch – Step 14**

15. Count two blocks to the right and one block up. Bring the needle up to the front of the fabric at the top right corner of the block.

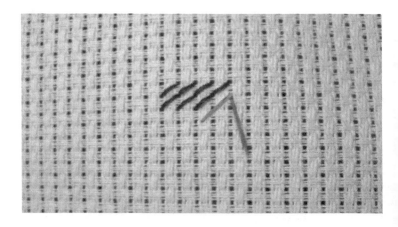

**Tent Stitch – Step 15**

16. Count one block down and one block to the left. Push the needle down through the fabric at the bottom left corner of the block.

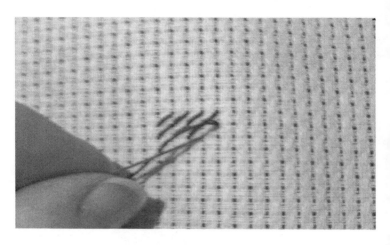

**Tent Stitch – Step 16**

17. The Tent Stitch is completed.

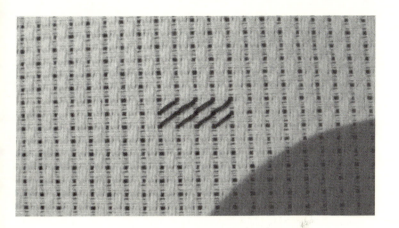

**Tent Stitch – Completed**

## *Irish Stitch*

- This stitch is also known as the Florentine Stitch or the Flame Stitch. It is used as a filler stitch. When completed, it looks like a zig zag design across your project.

### *Step-By-Step Action Steps*

1. Bring the needle up to the front of the fabric at the top left corner of the block.

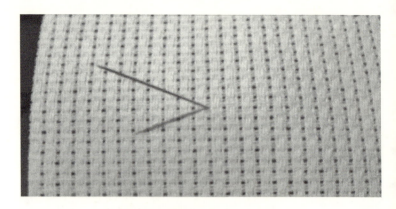

**Irish Stitch – Step 1**

2. Count down four blocks. Push the needle down through the fabric at the bottom right corner of the fourth block.

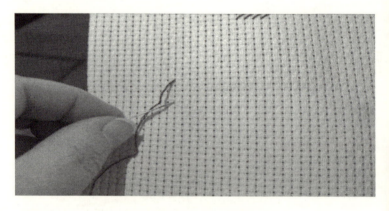

**Irish Stitch – Step 2**

3. Count one block to the right and six blocks up. Bring the needle up to the front of the fabric at the top left corner of the sixth block.

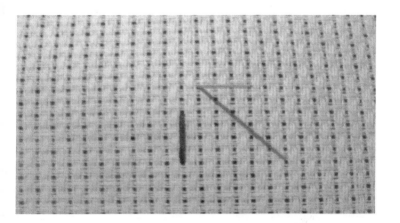

**Irish Stitch – Step 3**

4. Count four blocks down. Push the needle down through the fabric at the bottom right corner of the fourth block.

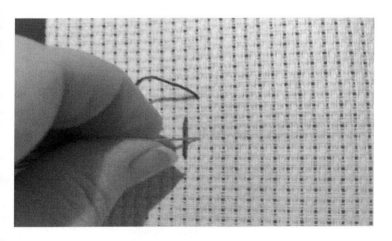

**Irish Stitch – Step 4**

5. Count one block to the right and six blocks up. Bring the needle up to the front of the fabric at the top left corner of the sixth block.

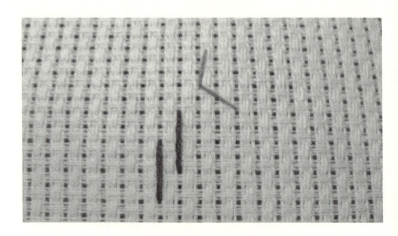

**Irish Stitch – Step 5**

6. Count four blocks straight down. Push the needle down through the fabric at the top left corner of the fourth block.

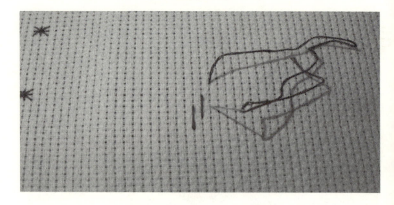

**Irish Stitch – Step 6**

7. Count one block to the right and six blocks up. Bring the needle up to the front of the fabric at the top left corner of the sixth block.

**Irish Stitch – Step 7**

8. Count four blocks straight down. Push the needle down through the fabric at the bottom right corner of the fourth block.

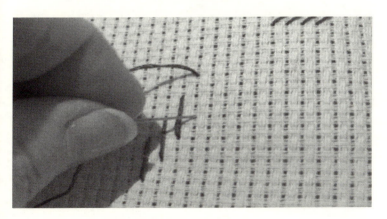

**Irish Stitch – Step 8**

9. Count one block to the right and two blocks up. Bring the needle up to the front of the fabric at the top left corner of the second block.

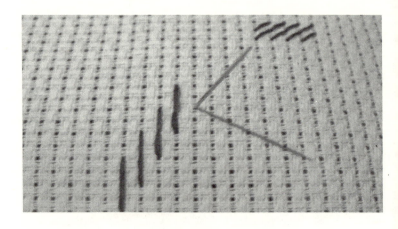

**Irish Stitch – Step 9**

10. Count four blocks straight down. Push the needle down through the fabric at the bottom right corner of the fourth block.

**Irish Stitch – Step 10**

11. Count one block to the right and two blocks up. Bring the needle up to the front of the fabric at the top left corner of the second block.

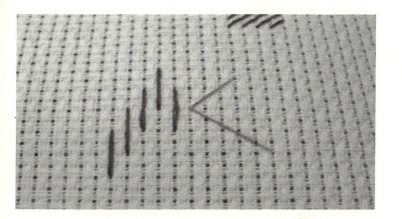

**Irish Stitch – Step 11**

12. Count four blocks straight down. Push the needle down through the fabric at the bottom right corner of the fourth block.

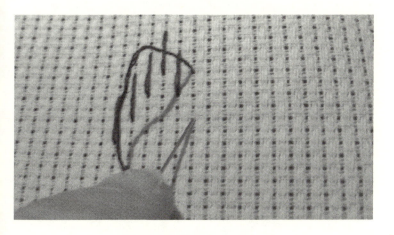

**Irish Stitch – Step 12**

13. Count one block to the right and two blocks up. Bring the needle up to the front of the fabric at the top left corner of the second block.

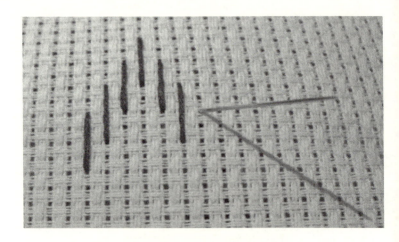

**Irish Stitch – Step 13**

14. Count four blocks straight down. Push the needle down through the fabric at the bottom right corner of the fourth block.

**Irish Stitch – Step 14**

15. Count one block to the right and two blocks up. Bring the needle up to the front of the fabric at the top left corner of the second block.

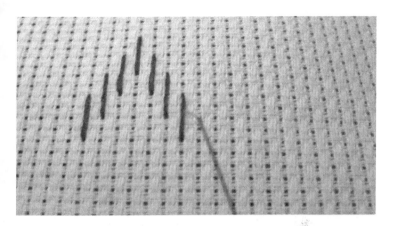

**Irish Stitch – Step 15**

16. Count four blocks straight up. Push the needle down through the fabric at the top right corner of the fourth block.

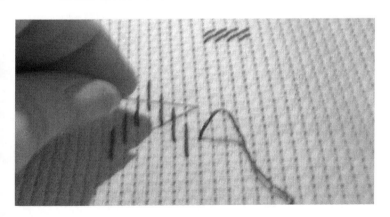

**Irish Stitch – Step 16**

17. Count one block to the right and two blocks down. Bring the needle up to the front of the fabric at the bottom left corner of the second block.

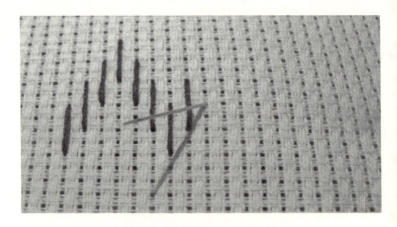

**Irish Stitch – Step 17**

18. Count four blocks straight up. Push the needle down through the fabric at the top right corner of the fourth block.

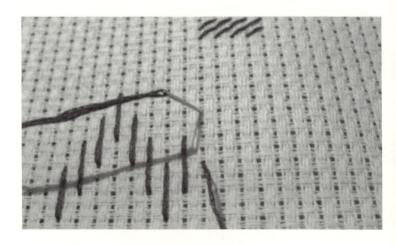

**Irish Stitch – Step 18**

19. The Irish Stitch is completed.

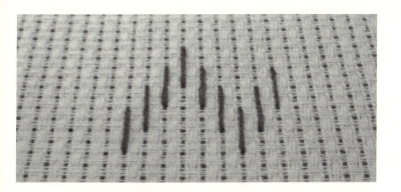

**Irish Stitch – Completed**

## *Rice Stitch*

- This stitch is a fancy cross stitch. It is used as a border or as background filler.

### *Step-By-Step Action Steps*

1. Bring the needle up to the front of the fabric at the top left corner of the block.

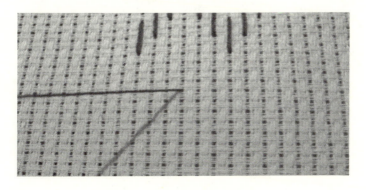

**Rice Stitch – Step 1**

2. Count four blocks to the right and four blocks down. Push the needle down through the fabric at the bottom right corner of the fourth block.

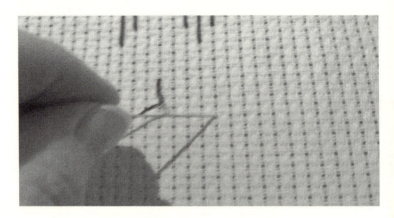

**Rice Stitch – Step 2**

3. Count four blocks to the left. Push the needle down through the fabric at the bottom left corner of the fourth block.

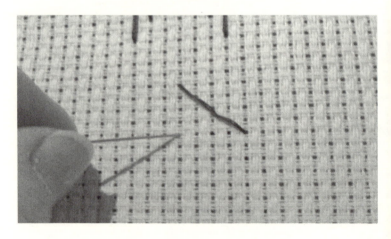

**Rice Stitch – Step 3**

4. Count four blocks up and four blocks to the right. Push the needle down through the fabric at the top right corner of the fourth block.

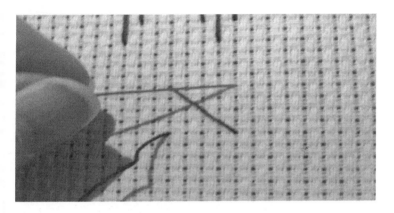

**Rice Stitch – Step 4**

5. Count two blocks to the left. Bring the needle up to the front of the fabric at the top left corner of the second block.

**Rice Stitch – Step 5**

6. Count two blocks to the right and two blocks down. Push the needle down through the fabric at the bottom right corner of the second block.

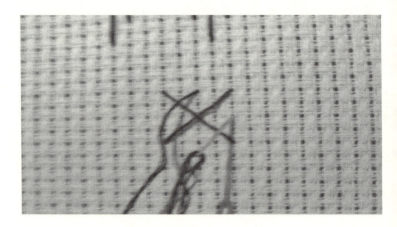

**Rice Stitch – Step 6**

7. Count four blocks to the left. Bring the needle to the front of the fabric at the bottom left corner of the fourth block.

**Rice Stitch – Step 7**

8. Count two blocks up and two blocks to the right. Push the needle down through the fabric at the bottom right corner of the second block.

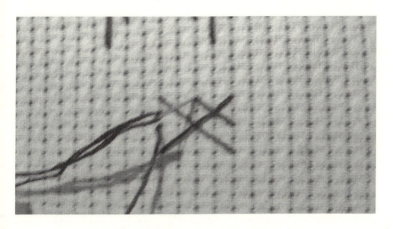

**Rice Stitch – Step 8**

9. Count four blocks straight down. Push the needle down through the fabric at the bottom right corner of the fourth block.

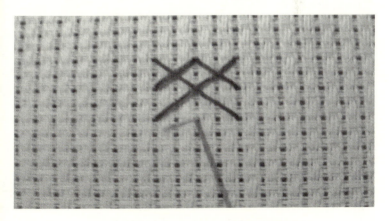

**Rice Stitch – Step 9**

10. Count two blocks to the left and two blocks up. Push the needle down through the fabric at the top left corner of the second block.

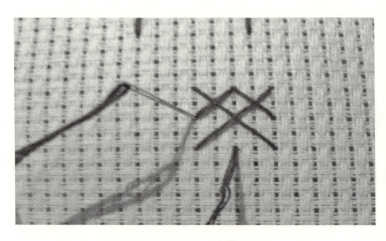

**Rice Stitch – Step 10**

11. Count two blocks down and two blocks to the right. Bring the needle to the front of the fabric at the bottom left corner of the second block.

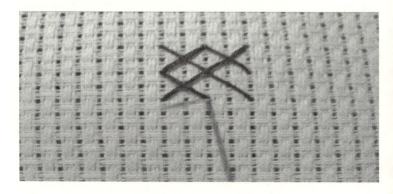

**Rice Stitch – Step 11**

12. Count two blocks to the right and two blocks up. Push the needle down through the fabric at the bottom left corner of the fourth block.

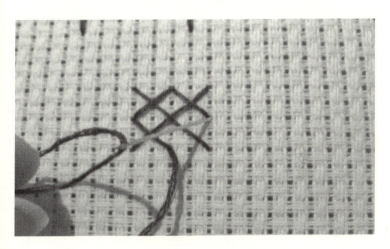

**Rice Stitch – Step 12**

13. The Rice Stitch is completed.

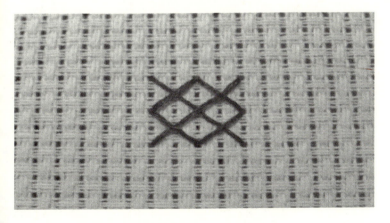

**Rice Stitch - Completed**

# Chapter 10: How To prepare a project for finishing

After you've spent all that time stitching your project, you will probably want to clean it before you hang it on your wall or present it as a gift. The fabric may have collected oils from your hands, dust particles from the air around you, and various other things that you don't even want to think about. If this happened, despite how clean you tried to keep it, don't stress about it. It happens to the best of us sometimes. Here's the best way to clean your project:

- Cold tap water and soap are the best.
    - If you have hard tap water, you'll want to use distilled water since the minerals in the hard water will eventually destroy your fabric.
    - Make sure the sink and/or containers you use to clean your finished piece are clean. You don't want to have leftover spaghetti sauce residue showing up on your fabric.
    - There are special detergents out there for cross stitch and embroidery fabrics, but regular detergents will do as long as they don't have additives such as fragrances, softeners, etc. Personally, I spend the extra money for the special fabric cleaner just so that I don't have to worry about looking for all the additives.
- Get the fabric wet with cold, running water.

- Put it in the sink or container with cold, soapy water and wash it gently. You don't want to scrub it because that can loosen your stitches or distort your fabric.

- Rinse and wash again. DO NOT WRING THE WATER OUT!!!! This can also pull the stitches and distort the fabric.

- Rinse the fabric three times.
    - You will want to watch for color bleeding from the thread (usually the reds), hoop marks (usually dirt and oil stains that collected where the hoop was holding the fabric for a long period), or any other stains while you are washing and rinsing.
    - If you see any of these stains, you will need to stop and concentrate on those areas, since you don't want those stains to dry or they will become permanent. If you can't get them out, you can be creative in covering them up with extra stitches to hide them, or you can add charms or buttons to enhance your design. For instance, if was a garden scene, you could add butterfly and bee buttons and charms to cover the stains. (You can find these buttons and charms at any craft store.)

- Take the fabric out from the last rinse cycle, letting the water drain from it naturally. DO NOT WRING THE WATER OUT!!!

- You'll want to put the fabric on a dry bath towel and roll both the towel and cross stitch fabric up together. Gently press on the towel roll so that excess water from the cross stitch fabric is absorbed into the towel.

    - Unroll the towel and fabric, and move it to a dry section of the towel or to a new dry towel. Repeat the rolling and pressing process until the fabric is no longer soaking wet.

- Open up the towel. Place the fabric with the project stitching face up on a dry section of the towel so that it can air dry until it is just damp.

- Once it is completely dry, you are ready to have it framed.

As a beginning stitcher, I would take my projects to the local craft store to have them professionally framed, simply because I didn't know how to do it as well as they did. They know how to do the matting, cut the glass, and put the frame together. Yes, it can be a bit expensive, but in the end it is worth it when you consider all the time and effort you put into the project yourself. Plus, I was usually giving my projects as gifts and I wanted them to look professional, which they wouldn't have if I had done the framing.

However, as time has gone on I now do my own framing. As you gain experience, you can too. It's just a matter of taking baby steps and learning how to the cross stitch first. Once you have that down (which won't take long), you'll be framing in no time.

# Conclusion

Some people may think that doing cross stitch is too complicated, but it can be easy and fun. Patterns range from easy for the beginner to those that are very intricate and detailed for the expert stitcher. At any rate, if you have been afraid to try cross stitch in the past, overcome your fears and give it a try. You might find that you enjoy it, if you just remember to take it one stitch at a time!

# About the Expert

Brenda Morris has been doing cross stitch for 37 years. After watching her grandmother and mother working with their needlework projects, she became interested in following in their footsteps. She started doing simple embroidery projects then moved to stamped cross stitch pieces. From there she branched out into counted cross stitch.

Brenda found that she preferred the challenge of the counted cross stitch to working with the pre-printed images used for stamped cross stitch. She began with the smaller, simpler counted patterns and worked her way up to the more complicated and intricate designs. She has even designed patterns for personal gifts for family and friends.

The best advice Brenda would offer to the beginning cross stitcher is, "Keep going, even when you get frustrated. Any stitch that goes in can be pulled out and be redone."

HowExpert publishes quick 'how to' guides on all topics from A to Z by everyday experts. Visit HowExpert.com to learn more.

# Recommended Resources

- HowExpert.com – Quick 'How To' Guides on All Topics from A to Z by Everyday Experts.
- HowExpert.com/free – Free HowExpert Email Newsletter.
- HowExpert.com/books – HowExpert Books
- HowExpert.com/courses – HowExpert Courses
- HowExpert.com/clothing – HowExpert Clothing
- HowExpert.com/membership – HowExpert Membership Site
- HowExpert.com/affiliates – HowExpert Affiliate Program
- HowExpert.com/writers – Write About Your #1 Passion/Knowledge/Expertise & Become a HowExpert Author.
- HowExpert.com/resources – Additional HowExpert Recommended Resources
- YouTube.com/HowExpert – Subscribe to HowExpert YouTube.
- Instagram.com/HowExpert – Follow HowExpert on Instagram.
- Facebook.com/HowExpert – Follow HowExpert on Facebook.

Made in the USA
Middletown, DE
29 June 2025